contents

Barbara Bush

RED, WHITE & BLUE COBBLER

1 can blueberry pie filling
1 can cherry pie filling

Place blueberry pie filling in bottom of 8" x 8" glass baking pan. Spread evenly and then place the cherry pie filling on top, smoothing to edges of pan. Place in 400 degree oven to heat while preparing topping.

Topping

1 cup flour
1 T. sugar
1 ½ tsp. baking powder

½ tsp. salt
3 T. shortening
½ cup milk

Mix dry ingredients and shortening until it is like fine crumbs. Stir in milk and drop by spoonfuls onto hot filling. Bake at 400 degrees for 25-30 minutes or until brown. Top with vanilla ice cream.

Our family has visited Boca Grande for years. We love the island and have made many happy memories during our trips to this sunny and family-oriented place.

Some of my favorite times included playing in family golf tournaments, and watching tennis tournaments between my George and our grandchildren. Another time George W. and our grandson Jeb Jr. raced to see who was the fastest runner. We all lined the street to cheer them on, watching as Jeb Jr. left George W. in the dust. What a fun day (especially for Jeb Jr.!).

Boca Grande is absolutely gorgeous, and through the years it has been kept up so well. I think of it as an unspoiled paradise. One group we can thank for that is The Boca Grande Woman's Club. The members of the club have worked tirelessly to keep the island beautiful and to help their neighbors. I especially applaud their good work to provide college scholarships to students. They are truly making a difference in many young lives, and all of the Bushes admire and thank them for their service.

Best wishes as you enjoy this cookbook!

Warmly,

Barbara Bush

the joys of cooking

I find contentment in my cooking.
I feel affection for my knives...
appreciation for my pots...
anticipation in recipes that challenge.

To braise or bake, sauté or steam?
There are so many choices
that open windows to the senses
and promise a culinary coup.

This is where tasting is tested;
flavors are savored;
seasonings become commitments...
where curry and saffron and cumin are king.

I chop, I slice, I dice
and seem to affirm some primordial need
that goes beyond appeasing hunger
and calls for creativity.

I savor kitchen smells... my culinary perfumes...
garlic sizzling in butter...
the aroma of a lively, bubbling sauce
that titillates my taste buds.

There is magic in fresh ingredients...
in a season's first offering...
and satisfaction when guests applaud
and when, at meal's end, I view their empty plates!

Love and integrity blend the process;
tradition too... in recipes handed down,
ideas exchanged... a sharing of passions;
a celebration of life.

I see communion in the love of food...
its preparation and its pleasure
and how, so often, it brings us, expectantly,
to the table and each other.

Fred Berger, Poet

hors d'oeuvres

boca **hearts of palm**

1 (14.4-ounce) can hearts of palm, drained and chopped

1 cup shredded mozzarella cheese

¾ cup mayonnaise

½ cup grated Parmesan cheese

¼ cup sour cream

1 green onion, minced

Preheat oven to 350°. Combine **hearts of palm,** mozzarella cheese, mayonnaise, Parmesan cheese, sour cream and onion. Spoon mixture into a lightly oiled 9-inch quiche dish or pie plate. Bake uncovered for 20 minutes or until hot and bubbly. Serve with crackers or Melba rounds; also delicious served as a sauce for broccoli, cauliflower or on a baked potato.

cheese stuffed dates with bacon

Makes 48

1 (10-ounce) box pitted dates

4 ounces Manchego or blue cheese

24 bacon slices, cut in half crosswise

Cut tip from end of each date, enlarging the opening slightly. Cut cheese into small stick-like pieces and stuff them into the center of the date. Wrap date with bacon and fasten with a toothpick. Dates can be refrigerated until ready to serve. Preheat broiler; place dates on baking sheet and broil until bacon is brown and crispy, turning once. Stuffed dates freeze well. Just thaw and broil.

CHEF TIP:

PLACING BLUE CHEESE IN FREEZER UNTIL IT HARDENS MAKES IT MUCH EASIER TO SLICE AND GRATE.

two season fig and cheese crostini

Makes 8 pieces

8 baguette slices, about ⅓-inch thick, lightly toasted

Summer Version

3 ounces Gorgonzola cheese, crumbled

4 small ripe fresh figs, thinly sliced

Preheat the broiler. Arrange the toasted baguette slices on a small baking sheet. Top each one with some crumbled Gorgonzola, dividing it evenly. Arrange the fig slices on top of the cheese, dividing them evenly. Broil the crostini until the cheese melts and bubbles along the edges, about 3 minutes.

NOTE:

CHOOSE FRESH FIGS THAT FEEL PLUMP AND HEAVY AND GIVE SLIGHTLY TO PRESSURE FROM YOUR FINGERTIP. THE SKIN SHOULD BE UNBLEMISHED.

Winter Version

½ cup dried mission figs, thinly sliced

½ cup ruby port

3 ounces Stilton cheese, crumbled

Freshly ground black pepper to taste

Combine the figs and port in a small heavy saucepan set over medium-low heat. Simmer until most of the liquid is gone, about 10 minutes. Preheat the broiler. Top each crostini with the Stilton cheese, dividing it evenly. Broil the crostini until the cheese melts and bubbles, about 2 minutes. Top with the figs, dividing them evenly. Garnish with a sprinkling of ground pepper.

mascarpone and pistachio toasts

Makes 18 slices

4 ounces mascarpone cheese, room temperature

18 slices (¼-inch thick) French baguette

⅓ cup pistachios, coarsely chopped

2 tablespoons honey

2 tablespoons julienned fresh basil

Preheat oven to 350°. Spread cheese on each bread slice. Place in a single layer on a 10 x 15 x 1-inch baking sheet. Sprinkle pistachios over cheese. Bake 10 to 12 minutes or until edges of bread are light brown. Drizzle honey over top of each toast. Garnish with basil.

marinated goat cheese with mixed olives

Serves 4 to 6

½ cup assorted pitted olives, coarsely chopped

3 sprigs fresh thyme

3 tablespoons extra virgin olive oil

½ teaspoon lemon zest

¼ teaspoon freshly ground black pepper

1 (4-ounce) goat cheese, plain or herb

Crackers

Place olives, thyme, olive oil, lemon zest and pepper in a saucepan. Heat on medium-low until fragrant. Do not boil or simmer. Cool to room temperature.

Place cheese in a small bowl and spoon oil mixture over cheese. Can be made ahead and refrigerated. Continue to spoon oil over the top.

To serve, bring cheese to room temperature and spoon olives over and around cheese. Serve with crackers.

feta cheese and walnut spread

Serves 16 to 20

8 ounces feta cheese, drained

2 tablespoons extra virgin olive oil

¾ cup Greek-style yogurt

Cayenne pepper to taste

¼ teaspoon kosher salt

1 cup walnut pieces, toasted

GARNISH: Chopped parsley

CHEF TIP:
RUB TOASTED WALNUTS IN A CLEAN DISH TOWEL TO REMOVE AS MUCH OF THE SLIGHTLY BITTER SKIN AS POSSIBLE.

In the bowl of a food processor, combine feta, oil, yogurt, cayenne and salt. Add walnuts and pulse, leaving walnuts slightly chunky. Sprinkle with parsley and serve with pita chips, crudités or spread on endive leaves.

handmade pita crisps

¾ **cup olive oil**

2 teaspoons paprika

10 (6-inch) pita pockets

Kosher salt to taste

Preheat oven to 350°. In a small bowl, stir together the olive oil and paprika. Using a sharp knife, halve each pita so that you have 2 circles and no pocket. Brush the rough sides of the pitas with the paprika oil and season generously with salt. Cut each pita half into 7 or 8 wedges and arrange them in a single layer on a large baking sheet. Bake in the middle of the oven until lightly browned and crisp, about 10 minutes. Cool on wire racks before serving.

The pita crisps can be made up to 2 days ahead of time and stored in zip-top plastic bags at room temperature.

warm bacon cheese spread

Serves 8 to 10

8 slices bacon, cooked until crisp and finely crumbled

¼ **cup coarsely crumbled round buttery crackers**

1 (8-ounce) package cream cheese, room temperature

4 ounces Swiss cheese, shredded

½ **cup mayonnaise**

3 to 4 green onions, chopped

Round buttery crackers

Preheat oven to 350°. Mix together bacon and cracker crumbs; set aside. Combine softened cream cheese, Swiss cheese, mayonnaise and green onions. Oil a pie plate or quiche dish and fill with cheese mixture. Bake 15 minutes. Remove from oven and top with bacon and cracker mixture. Bake 10 minutes longer. Serve with crackers.

mousse with the blues

1 (3-ounce) package cream cheese

3 ounces blue cheese

1 teaspoon dried thyme

1 tablespoon port wine or bourbon

Freshly ground black pepper to taste

Crackers or cherry tomatoes

Place the cheeses in the bowl of a food processor fitted with the steel blade. Soak thyme in the port or bourbon for five minutes; add this mixture to cheeses along with pepper. Process until smooth. Serve with crackers or as a filling for cherry tomatoes.

CHEF TIP:

THIS MOUSSE CAN BE SPREAD ON SLICES OF HAM, ROLLED AND SLICED INTO PINWHEELS OR USED AS A TOPPING FOR GRILLED HAMBURGERS.

mangrove mango chutney mold

Serves 12

12 ounces cream cheese, room temperature

3 tablespoons mayonnaise

3 tablespoons chopped peanuts

3 tablespoons chopped raisins

3 slices bacon, cooked until crisp and crumbled

2 teaspoons chopped green onions

2 teaspoons curry powder

½ cup shredded coconut

1 cup chopped mango chutney

Crackers or small ginger cookies

Combine the cream cheese with the mayonnaise, peanuts, raisins, bacon, green onions and curry powder in the bowl of a food processor; pulse until ingredients are coarsely chopped. Pour into a lightly oiled 3-cup mold and chill overnight. Remove from the mold and cover with the coconut and mango chutney. Serve with crackers or ginger cookies.

sunset pinwheels

1 sheet frozen puff pastry, thawed

4 ounces Roquefort or other blue cheese

1 egg, lightly beaten with 1 teaspoon cold water

Preheat oven to 400°. Open sheet of puff pastry on a floured surface. Flatten slightly with a rolling pin, creating a rectangle approximately 8 x 12-inches. Crumble the blue cheese on the sheet, leaving a 1-inch border all around. Roll up the pastry the long way. Cut into 12 slices with a sharp knife. Place them on a nonstick baking sheet (or a parchment paper-lined baking sheet). Brush with egg wash and bake 10 to 12 minutes or until puffed and golden.

bike trail snack mix

Makes 13 cups

6 cups crispy rice cereal squares

3 cups roasted mixed salted nuts
   (almonds, cashews, pistachios and peanuts)

1½ cups Asian rice cracker mix

1½ cups sesame sticks

1½ cups pretzel nuggets or mini pretzels

½ cup butter

¼ cup pure maple syrup

3 tablespoons soy sauce

1½ teaspoons Thai red curry paste

Kosher salt and freshly ground black pepper to taste

NOTE:
THIS MIX MAKES A GREAT
HOSTESS GIFT.

Preheat oven to 275°. In a large bowl, combine the cereal with the nuts, rice cracker mix, sesame sticks and pretzels. In a medium saucepan, combine the butter, maple syrup, soy sauce and curry paste. Bring to a simmer, whisking to dissolve the curry paste. Pour the mixture over the snack mix and toss to coat completely. Season generously with salt and pepper; spread on 2 large rimmed baking sheets. Bake for 35 minutes, stirring 2 or 3 times and shifting the sheets in the oven, until nearly dry and toasted. Let cool completely, stirring occasionally.

salsa cheesecake

1 (8-ounce) package cream cheese, room temperature

1 (8-ounce) package light cream cheese, room temperature

½ cup grated Romano cheese

1½ cups grated Monterey Jack cheese or pepper Jack cheese

2 cups light sour cream, divided

1 tablespoon flour

3 eggs

1½ tablespoons minced green onion

8 ounces medium or hot salsa

4 ounces canned diced green chiles, drained

GARNISH: 6 ounces guacamole

⅓ cup chopped red bell pepper

Chopped fresh cilantro

Tortilla chips or crackers

Preheat oven to 350°. In large bowl, combine cream cheese, light cream cheese, Romano and Monterey Jack cheeses. With an electric mixer, beat until light and fluffy. Mix in 1 cup sour cream and flour; add eggs all at once. Mix well. Stir in green onion, salsa and chiles.

Pour into a 9-inch springform pan. Place pan on baking sheet in center of oven. Bake 40 to 45 minutes until center is nearly set; remove from oven. Spread remaining 1 cup light sour cream over top of hot cheesecake. Cool on a rack. Refrigerate, covered, at least 4 hours.

To serve, remove sides of pan. If desired, swirl guacamole around outer edge of cheesecake. Sprinkle guacamole with red bell pepper and cilantro. Serve with tortilla chips or crackers.

guacamole with roasted chili, cumin and feta

Makes 2 cups

1 small fresh green New Mexico or poblano chili

1 lime

3 avocados, firm-ripe, peeled and pitted

3 green onions, chopped

5 tablespoons chopped fresh cilantro

¼ teaspoon ground cumin

Kosher salt to taste

½ cup medium-diced tomato

Slivered radishes

Crumbled feta cheese

Corn tortilla chips

NOTE:

THE TWO MOST FREQUENTLY MARKETED AVOCADO VARIETIES ARE THE PEBBLY TEXTURED, ALMOST BLACK HASS AND THE GREEN FUERTE, WHICH HAS A THIN, SMOOTH SKIN. AVOCADOS RIPEN BEST OFF THE TREE. PLACE SEVERAL IN A PAPER BAG AND SET ASIDE AT ROOM TEMPERATURE FOR SEVERAL DAYS TO SPEED THE RIPENING PROCESS.

On a gas stove, turn a burner to high and set the chili directly over the flame; turn it with tongs, until completely charred, 5 to 8 minutes. Alternatively, place chili on baking sheet and char under broiler. Put the chili in a paper bag. Close tightly and set aside to steam until the skin is loosened and easy to remove. When cool enough to handle, peel, seed and finely chop.

Finely grate the zest from the lime and then squeeze the juice. Put the avocados in a bowl and coarsely mash with a potato masher. Stir in the lime zest and 2 tablespoons of the lime juice along with the green onions, cilantro, cumin and $1/2$ teaspoon salt. Season to taste with additional salt and lime juice; then fold in the chili and tomato.

Spoon the guacamole into a bowl and top with radishes and feta. Serve with tortilla chips.

For quicker preparation, substitute canned green chiles.

spicy bourbon pecans

Makes 4 cups

1 pound pecan halves

½ cup bourbon

½ cup sugar

½ teaspoon bitters

1 tablespoon Worcestershire sauce

1 tablespoon canola oil

½ teaspoon cayenne pepper

½ teaspoon kosher salt

¼ teaspoon freshly ground black pepper

1 teaspoon cumin

Preheat oven to 325°. Put pecans in a saucepan; cover with water. Bring to a boil over high heat. Boil 1 minute; drain and rinse with cold water. Bring the bourbon to a boil in a saucepan large enough to hold the nuts. When the bourbon is reduced to $\frac{1}{4}$ cup, mix in the sugar, bitters, Worcestershire sauce and oil. Fold in the drained pecans. Mix thoroughly and let stand 10 minutes.

Spread the nuts on a rimmed baking sheet and bake for 35 minutes, tossing nuts every 10 minutes. All liquid should be absorbed.

In a bowl that will hold the nuts, combine cayenne, salt, pepper and cumin; mix in the nuts. When well combined, return to the baking sheet until cool and dry. Store in a covered container or freeze for later use.

If nuts do not dry and become crisp, they can be returned to the oven briefly.

"olive you forever" stuffed olives

Makes 24

24 large green olives, pitted

½ cup bottled Italian dressing

24 pepperoni slices

Combine olives and Italian dressing; stir to combine. Marinate in refrigerator for 24 hours, stirring occasionally.

Before serving, drain olives thoroughly. Roll pepperoni slices into a cone shape. Stuff each olive with pepperoni; insert a toothpick in each one. Place olives in a row on an olive dish or plate and serve.

party peppers

Makes 24 hors d'oeuvres

1 box red, yellow and orange miniature sweet peppers

8 ounces goat cheese

2 ounces finely chopped pistachios or toasted almonds

Kosher salt to taste

Zest of one lemon

GARNISH: Whole pistachios or almonds

COMPLIMENTS OF:

KIM NEWLIN, PROPRIETOR

NEWLIN'S MAINELY GOURMET

BOCA GRANDE, FLORIDA

Heat oven to 400°. Split the peppers lengthwise, remove seeds and membrane. Roast on a baking sheet sprayed with olive oil until soft but still holding their shape. Cool slightly.

Cream the cheese, fold in the nuts, season with salt and pipe or spoon into peppers. Sprinkle with lemon zest and garnish each with a whole nut.

caesar dipping sauce and crudités

Makes 1¼ cups

1 to 2 teaspoons minced garlic

¼ teaspoon kosher salt

1 cup mayonnaise

1 cup grated Parmesan cheese

1 teaspoon drained and mashed anchovies, or to taste

3 tablespoons fresh lemon juice

½ cup finely chopped flat-leaf parsley

Freshly ground black pepper to taste

CRUDITÉS: cauliflower, red and yellow bell pepper strips, carrot sticks,
broccoli, blanched asparagus and Brussels sprouts or
cooked shrimp.

In a bowl, mash together garlic and salt. Add mayonnaise, Parmesan
cheese, anchovies, lemon juice, parsley and black pepper. Mix
together. Refrigerate at least 4 hours. Serve with crudités.

party-pretty tomato crostini

Serves 4

3 plum tomatoes, cut into ¼-inch dice

4 ounces goat cheese, cut into bits

1 garlic clove, minced

2 tablespoons extra virgin olive oil

Kosher salt and freshly ground black pepper to taste

Fresh chopped basil

French baguette slices, toasted

Preheat oven to 350°. Combine the plum tomatoes, goat cheese,
garlic, olive oil, salt and pepper. Bake in a shallow ovenproof dish for
20 minutes. Sprinkle with chopped fresh basil. Serve with baguette
slices.

crispy sesame eggplant

¾ **cup saltine cracker crumbs**

½ **cup grated Parmesan cheese**

¼ **cup sesame seeds**

Kosher salt and freshly ground black pepper to taste

1 medium eggplant (about 1¼ pounds)

Mayonnaise

Preheat oven to 400°. Oil or spray 2 baking sheets. Stir the cracker crumbs, Parmesan cheese, sesame seeds, salt and pepper together in a small bowl.

Cut off the stem and cap of the eggplant and peel. Cut it into ¹/₂-inch thick slices. Spread both sides of each slice with mayonnaise. Dip each side into the crumb mixture, pressing lightly so that it adheres. Cut each slice in quarters, making four triangles. Place them on the prepared baking sheets. Bake 10 to 12 minutes until the undersides are golden. Turn the triangles over and bake 5 to 7 minutes longer, or until they are golden on both sides. Serve warm or at room temperature.

The baked triangles can be frozen. Do not defrost them. Reheat frozen at 400° for 4 to 5 minutes, or until hot.

NOTE:

A GOOD EGGPLANT SHOULD BE HEAVY FOR ITS SIZE AND SMOOTH SKINNED WITH NO SOFT OR BROWN SPOTS. EGGPLANTS BECOME BITTER WITH AGE AND SHOULD BE USED WITHIN 1 OR 2 DAYS OF PURCHASE.

tipsy tomatoes

1 pint grape tomatoes

½ **cup tequila**

2 tablespoons coarse sea salt

Arrange grape tomatoes on a plate. Put tequila in one small bowl and sea salt in another small bowl. Serve with toothpicks.

To eat, dip tomato into the tequila, then into the salt.

NOTE:

THIS COMBINATION OF TOMATOES, TEQUILA AND SEA SALT MAKES A NOVEL, QUICK AND EASY HORS D'OEUVRE.

petite lobster salad sliders

1 small red bell pepper, finely diced

1 small red onion, finely diced

2 green onions, thinly sliced

1 celery rib, finely diced

1 lemon, zest removed and juiced

¾ cup mayonnaise

1 pound lobster meat, cooked and diced

Cherry tomatoes, thinly sliced

Lettuce

Small buns

COMPLIMENTS OF:

CHEF JACQUES BOUDREAU

THE LOOSE CABOOSE

BOCA GRANDE, FLORIDA

Combine red bell pepper, red onion, green onions, celery, lemon zest, lemon juice, mayonnaise and lobster meat. Chill. Serve lobster salad, tomatoes and lettuce on small buns.

smoked mullet pâté

8 ounces cream cheese, room temperature

¼ cup coarsely chopped onion

¾ teaspoon horseradish

½ teaspoon lemon juice

1 teaspoon Dijon mustard (optional)

1 cup (7-ounces) smoked mullet pieces
   (or other smoked fish such as trout, blue fish, mackerel)

1 tablespoon capers

Crackers

NOTE:

MULLET CAN BE FOUND YEAR-ROUND IN MOST SOUTH ATLANTIC AND GULF WATERS. IT HAS FIRM WHITE FLESH WITH A MILD, NUTLIKE FLAVOR. IT IS FREQUENTLY SMOKED IN THE SOUTH.

In the bowl of a food processor, combine cream cheese, onion, horseradish, lemon juice and mustard; process until blended. Add ¹/₂ of the smoked fish and process until almost smooth. Add remaining smoked fish and the capers. Pulse briefly, leaving the fish slightly chunky. Chill for at least 2 hours. Serve with crackers.

mussels vinaigrette

½ cup extra virgin olive oil

3 tablespoons red wine vinegar

1 teaspoon capers, roughly chopped

1 tablespoon minced onion

1 tablespoon minced pimiento

1 tablespoon minced parsley

Kosher salt and freshly ground black pepper to taste

1 lemon slice

2 dozen black mussels, beards removed and mussels scrubbed

For the vinaigrette, whisk together the oil and vinegar. Add the capers, onion, pimiento, parsley, salt and pepper. Set aside.

Place 1 cup water in a skillet with the lemon slice. Add the mussels and bring to a boil. Remove the mussels as they open; cool. Discard any mussels that do not open after cooking. Remove the meat from the shells and mix it into the vinaigrette (saving half of the shells). Cover and refrigerate mussels overnight. Clean the reserved shells well; place them in a plastic bag and refrigerate.

Before serving, return the mussels to their shells and spoon a small amount of the vinaigrette over each one.

This recipe adapts well for part of a tapas menu.

fingerling potatoes and smoked salmon

12 fingerling potatoes (about 1 pound), halved lengthwise

1½ tablespoons olive oil

Kosher salt to taste

4 ounces thinly sliced smoked salmon

½ cup crème fraîche or sour cream

1 tablespoon caviar or capers

Freshly ground black pepper to taste

Preheat oven to 425°. On a rimmed baking sheet, toss potatoes in olive oil and salt. Bake for 20 minutes or until golden brown and tender. Let cool.

Arrange pieces of smoked salmon on potatoes; top each with a dollop of crème fraîche, some caviar or capers and a sprinkling of pepper.

smoked salmon and fennel crostini

½ cup chopped fennel bulb

¼ cup chopped green onions

1 tablespoon extra virgin olive oil

2 teaspoons chopped fresh dill

1 teaspoon grated lemon zest

1½ tablespoons fresh lemon juice

1 teaspoon freshly ground black pepper

¾ pound smoked salmon, cut into thin strips or coarsely chopped

48 French baguette slices, ½-inch thick, toasted

½ cup Boursin cheese

GARNISH: Fresh chopped dill

Combine the fennel, green onions, olive oil, dill, lemon zest, lemon juice, pepper and salmon. Cover and chill at least 1 hour.

Spread toast slice with cheese. Top each with 1 tablespoon salmon mixture; sprinkle with dill.

smoked salmon, cucumber and dill mousse

1 pound smoked salmon (preferably unsliced), cut into
 ¼-inch dice, divided

2 cups diced seedless cucumber

¼ cup chopped fresh dill

⅓ cup finely chopped red onion, soaked in ice water to cover,
 drained and patted dry

2¼ cups sour cream

3 tablespoons fresh lemon juice

1 tablespoon grated lemon zest

2 tablespoons cold water

1 envelope unflavored gelatin

Kosher salt and freshly ground black pepper to taste

NOTE:

THIS MOUSSE IS A DELIGHTFUL
COOL SUMMER LUNCH SERVED
ON A BED OF LETTUCE WITH
LEMON RINGS AND CUCUMBER
RIBBONS.

Lightly oil an 8 x 2-inch round cake pan and line it with plastic wrap.
Spread 1¼ cups salmon evenly in cake pan. In a bowl, stir together
remaining salmon, cucumber, dill, onion, sour cream, lemon juice
and zest until well combined.

Put cold water in a small heatproof cup and sprinkle gelatin over
it. Put cup in a pan and add enough hot water to pan to reach
halfway up side of cup. Heat gently until gelatin is dissolved and
then stir into the salmon-cucumber mixture. Season with salt and
pepper. Spoon over diced salmon in cake pan. Chill mousse,
covered with plastic wrap, at least 6 hours and up to three days.

Invert pan over a serving plate and remove plastic wrap. Serve
chilled.

smoked salmon roll

8 ounces smoked salmon, thinly sliced

5 ounces Boursin cheese

½ red pepper, sliced into long thin strips

3 green onions, sliced lengthwise into strips

1 tablespoon capers

Crackers

GARNISH: Fresh chopped dill

COMPLIMENTS OF:

CHEF PATTY KITCHEN

THE GRAPEVINE

BOCA GRANDE, FLORIDA

Put parchment paper on a cutting board. Place salmon slices on paper, overlapping and creating a rectangle. Spread with Boursin cheese. Lay red pepper strips on cheese, the long way. Lay green onion strips on top of peppers; sprinkle with capers. With longest edge of paper closest to you, roll salmon into a jellyroll shape. Wrap tightly in parchment paper, twisting the ends to seal. Chill for at least 4 hours. Slice and serve on crackers; sprinkle with dill.

wasabi crab chips

Makes approximately 30 hors d'oeuvres

1 (8-ounce) package cream cheese, room temperature

4 teaspoons wasabi paste or to taste

Potato chips seasoned with black pepper and sea salt

1 pound lump crabmeat

Green onion tops, thinly sliced

Pickled ginger, finely slivered

NOTE:

WASABI IS THE JAPANESE VERSION OF HORSERADISH. IT IS USED TO MAKE A GREEN-COLORED CONDIMENT THAT HAS A SHARP, PUNGENT, FIERY FLAVOR. WASABI IS AVAILABLE IN PASTE AND POWDER FORM.

Thoroughly combine cream cheese and wasabi paste.

Select chips that are as flat as possible. Spread a teaspoon of cream cheese mixture on each chip and top with crabmeat. Sprinkle with green onion and place a piece of ginger on top; serve immediately.

thor's gravlax with mustard sauce

Marinated Salmon

3 to 4 pounds salmon
   (2 "matching" fillets, approximately 1½ to 2 pounds each)

⅔ cup kosher salt

½ cup sugar

20 white peppercorns, crushed

2 (1-ounce) packages fresh dill, plus extra for garnish

Crackers (preferably all natural, whole grain, crisp bread crackers)
   or thin, dark pumpernickel bread

Mustard Sauce

½ cup Dijon mustard

2 teaspoons dry mustard

6 tablespoons sugar

¼ cup white wine vinegar

⅔ cup extra virgin olive oil

6 tablespoons chopped fresh dill

NOTE:

GRAVLAX IS A SWEDISH SPECIALTY OF RAW SALMON CURED IN A SALT, SUGAR AND DILL MIXTURE. IT IS SLICED PAPER-THIN AND SERVED ON DARK BREAD AS AN APPETIZER, ON AN OPEN-FACED SANDWICH OR AS PART OF A SMORGASBORD. IT IS COMMONLY ACCOMPANIED WITH A MUSTARD DILL SAUCE.

To prepare the salmon, combine salt, sugar and pepper and rub ¼ of mixture thoroughly into both sides of each fillet. Place ¼ of the dill in bottom of a rectangular glass dish. Place one fillet on top of dill, skin side down. Place ½ of the dill on top of fillet. Pour all remaining salt mixture over the dill. Place second fillet on top, skin side up, simulating a sandwich. Top with remaining dill. Cover with plastic wrap. Place a weight on top of the salmon and refrigerate for 18 to 20 hours, turning the "sandwich" once or twice. Remove all dill and salt mixture. Slice salmon thinly and serve with crackers or bread and Mustard Sauce. Garnish with fresh dill sprigs.

To prepare mustard sauce, combine the Dijon mustard, dry mustard, sugar and vinegar in a small bowl. Slowly whisk in the oil and stir in the chopped dill.

chorizo banderillas

Makes 8 hors d'oeuvres

2 slices firm sandwich bread

Butter, room temperature

1 hard-cooked egg, sliced

3 ounce chorizo sausage, skin removed, cut into 8 (½-inch) slices

8 rolled anchovies

8 pimiento-stuffed green Spanish olives

Toast the bread very lightly, remove the crusts and spread with butter. Cut into 8 squares or cut 8 small rounds with a cutter. Cover each bread piece with a slice of egg, a slice of chorizo, an anchovy and top with the olive. Spear everything together with a toothpick. The banderillas can be prepared ahead.

NOTE:

BANDERILLAS ARE TAPAS, TIDBITS OF FOOD WHICH ARE SKEWERED ON TOOTHPICKS IN STACKS CREATING COLORFUL AND INTERESTING BLENDS OF FLAVORS. THE TRICK TO EATING A BANDERILLA IS TO PUT EVERYTHING THAT IS ON THE TOOTHPICK IN YOUR MOUTH AT ONCE SO THAT THE FLAVORS OF EACH INGREDIENT MERGE WITH THE REST.

The early history of Boca Grande, the town center of Gasparilla Island—a nod to the legendary pirate, Jose Gaspar, who supposedly buried hundreds of pounds of gold on the island—is well documented; the lore is dependent entirely upon the person telling the tales. Around 800 AD, the island was a veritable playground for the Calusa Indians. In the 16th century, Spanish explorers began trading with the Calusas, and through the years, various treaties between the Spanish governors and the king of the Calusas were signed and broken. The advent of European diseases and capture by other Indian tribes for slave trade began a slow demise of the tribe. Despite their strong nature-oriented belief in eternal spirits, by 1750 the Calusas are reported to have become extinct.

shrimp bruschetta al limoncello

24 French baguette slices

½ cup olive oil, divided

4 garlic cloves, thinly sliced

2 shallots, finely chopped

24 large shrimp, peeled and deveined

¼ cup fresh lemon juice

1 cup limoncello liqueur

Kosher salt and freshly ground black pepper to taste

GARNISH: Chopped fresh parsley

            Lemon zest

NOTE:
LIMONCELLO IS AN ITALIAN
LIQUEUR INFUSED WITH LEMON
RINDS.

Brush baguette slices with 2 tablespoons olive oil. Grill or toast bread slices until golden; arrange on a platter. Set aside.

In a large skillet, over medium-high heat, add remaining 6 tablespoons olive oil; sauté garlic and shallots 1 minute or until light golden brown. Add shrimp and sauté 2 to 3 minutes or until shrimp turn bright pink. Turn shrimp and cook 1 additional minute. Remove shrimp with a slotted spoon. Add lemon juice and limoncello to the skillet; cook over high heat until mixture is reduced by ⅔, about 2 minutes. Return shrimp to mixture, stirring until shrimp are coated. Remove from heat; add salt and pepper to taste. Spoon 1 shrimp with sauce onto each toast. Garnish with parsley and lemon zest.

chinese shrimp and scallion dumplings

¾ **pound medium shrimp, peeled, deveined and finely chopped**

3 **tablespoons canola oil**

1 **tablespoon minced garlic**

¾ **tablespoon minced ginger**

1½ **teaspoons soy sauce**

3 **green onions, finely chopped**

¼ **teaspoon kosher salt**

36 **dumpling or wonton wrappers**

ACCOMPANIMENTS: Asian-style hot mustard and reduced-sodium soy sauce for dipping

Stir together shrimp, oil, garlic, ginger, soy sauce, green onions and salt. Put a rounded teaspoon of filling in the center of a wrapper. Lightly brush edge of wrapper with water, then fold in half (diagonally if square) and press to seal. Form a tortellini shape by moistening 1 corner and bringing 2 corners together, pressing them. Form remaining dumplings.

Cook dumplings in 2 batches in a medium pot of gently simmering water until filling is just cooked, about 3 minutes per batch. Transfer with a slotted spoon to a platter. Keep warm, covered. Serve with dipping sauces.

NOTE:

DUMPLINGS CAN ALSO BE COOKED IN A STEAMER. THE CHINESE WAY IS TO LINE THE STEAMER WITH LETTUCE LEAVES AND PLACE THE DUMPLINGS ON TOP. OVER BOILING WATER, THESE WOULD COOK IN 5 MINUTES.

thai pork dumplings

Dumpling Sauce

⅔ cup soy sauce

⅓ cup rice wine vinegar

½ teaspoon sesame oil

2 tablespoons chopped green onions

Grated fresh ginger to taste

COMPLIMENTS OF:

CHEF PATRICK VOLLMER

PATRICK'S THAI BISTRO

AND SUSHI BAR

BOCA GRANDE, FLORIDA

Dumplings

1 cup cabbage, finely shredded

½ cup green onions, finely chopped, including white and green ends

1 tablespoon soy sauce

1 tablespoon oyster sauce

½ tablespoon grated fresh ginger

½ tablespoon minced garlic

½ tablespoon cornstarch

Splash dry white wine

½ tablespoon kosher salt

Freshly ground black pepper to taste

½ pound ground pork

40 pot sticker round wrappers

1 tablespoon sesame oil

1 to 1½ cups chicken stock

For the sauce, combine soy sauce, vinegar, oil, green onions and ginger. Set aside.

For the dumplings, mix together cabbage, green onions, soy sauce, oyster sauce, ginger, garlic, cornstarch, white wine, salt and pepper. You can do this in a food processor or by hand. Mix in pork by hand and refrigerate 15 minutes to set.

Fill pot sticker wrappers with ½ tablespoon of filling. Moisten edge of half of wrapper with cold water and fold in half creasing with finger. Heat oil in sauté pan. Cook dumplings in 3 batches. Brown on one side and turn over; add ⅓ to ½ cup chicken stock or water to each batch. Cover and steam over medium heat until liquid evaporates, about 5 minutes to cook pork. Serve immediately with the sauce.

charred beef with watercress vinaigrette

Makes 20 hors d'oeuvres

Charred Beef

1 (3 to 5 pound) sirloin strip, trimmed

Watercress Vinaigrette

¼ cup sherry wine vinegar

2 to 3 tablespoons Dijon mustard

½ to ¾ cup extra virgin olive oil

1 bunch fresh watercress, chopped

Kosher salt and freshly ground black pepper to taste

Toasted French baguette slices

Place sirloin strip in a very hot skillet and char on each side. Wrap tightly in a clean kitchen towel or cheese cloth. Refrigerate for 24 hours.

To prepare vinaigrette, whisk vinegar into mustard. Add olive oil slowly, whisking. Stir in watercress, salt and pepper.

To serve, slice beef paper thin and lay out on a platter. Drizzle with vinaigrette and serve with toasted baguette slices.

heavenly little cheeseburgers

1½ pounds ground chuck

Kosher salt and freshly ground black pepper to taste

40 (1½-inch) bread rounds cut from firm bread, lightly toasted

Mustard, ketchup and mayonnaise

40 (1-inch) sliced Cheddar cheese rounds

GARNISH: Dill pickle slices

Mix ground chuck with salt and pepper, and form into 1½-inch patties. Refrigerate.

Just before serving, spread bread rounds with any combination of mustard, ketchup and/or mayonnaise. Place a little burger on each bread round and broil for 2 to 3 minutes. Remove from oven, top with cheese round and broil until just beginning to melt, about 30 seconds. Add a small slice of dill pickle and skewer with a toothpick. Serve hot.

These burgers are delicious made in any size. A full size one makes a scrumptious lunch.

In the late 1800's most of Gasparilla Island was covered by palmettos, thick with rattlesnakes. The community consisted of four buildings, a working lighthouse and a shipping wharf. After the discovery of high-grade phosphate near the Peace River, the American Agricultural Chemical Company of Boston combined with The Peace River Phosphate Mining Company, and with the Charlotte Harbor and Northern Railroad, to create one of the first conglomerates of the U.S. But, as the CH&N trains began to rumble down the center of the Island to off-load phosphate to ships from all over the world, the local islanders—not sharing in the revenues—nicknamed the CH&N operation, *The Cold, Hungry, and Naked.*

breakfast, brunch & breads

strata with spinach, feta and bacon

¼ cup butter

5 garlic cloves, finely chopped

2 (10-ounce) boxes frozen chopped spinach, thawed, drained and
    squeezed dry

12 ounces slab bacon, preferably applewood-smoked, cut into
    ¼-inch cubes

12 ounces feta cheese, drained and crumbled

6 eggs

2½ cups half & half

1 teaspoon kosher salt

½ teaspoon freshly ground black pepper

¼ teaspoon crushed red pepper flakes

1 loaf French bread, bottom crust trimmed, cut into 1-inch chunks
    (approximately 6 cups)

½ cup grated Parmesan cheese

Butter a 9 x 13 x 2-inch baking dish. Put butter in a skillet and set over low heat. Add garlic and cook, stirring often without browning, for 3 minutes. Add the spinach and cook, tossing and stirring often, for 2 minutes. Remove and transfer to a medium bowl.

Wipe out skillet, add bacon and set over medium heat. Cook, stirring once or twice, until bacon is crisp and brown, about 15 to 20 minutes. With a slotted spoon, transfer bacon to bowl with the spinach mixture. Reserve 1 tablespoon of the bacon drippings. Add feta to bowl with bacon and spinach mixture and stir to combine.

In a large bowl, whisk eggs. Whisk in half & half, reserved bacon drippings, salt, black pepper and crushed red pepper. Scatter half the bread cubes in prepared baking dish. Spread half the spinach mixture evenly over the bread. Sprinkle half the Parmesan over the spinach. Repeat the layers. Pour egg mixture evenly over all. Cover casserole with plastic wrap and weigh it down to keep bread immersed in egg mixture. Refrigerate for at least 8 hours or overnight. Bring to room temperature before baking.

Preheat oven to 400°. Bake strata in middle of oven until the top is browned and the filling is set in the center, 40 to 55 minutes. Let strata rest on a rack for at least 5 minutes. Serve warm or hot.

goat cheese frittata

Serves 4 to 6

8 eggs

½ cup milk

Kosher salt and freshly ground black pepper to taste

1 tomato, diced

2 tablespoons chopped chives

2 teaspoons butter

5½ ounces goat cheese

Preheat oven to 375°. Mix together eggs, milk, salt, pepper, tomato and chives. Melt butter in ovenproof nonstick skillet. Add egg mixture and cook over medium heat until bottom is set and the edges start to pull away from the pan, 3 to 4 minutes. Top with heaping tablespoons of goat cheese. Bake for 10 minutes.

one perfect bloody mary

Serves 1

1 over-flowing jigger vodka

6 ounces chilled tomato-clam juice

1½ teaspoons Worcestershire sauce

¼ teaspoon seasoned salt

¼ lemon

Hot pepper sauce to taste

GARNISH: additional seasoned salt

Place ice in a 12-ounce tumbler. Add vodka, tomato-clam juice, Worcestershire sauce and seasoned salt; squeeze juice from the lemon into the glass, drop in lemon piece and stir well. Top with a light sprinkle of seasoned salt.

roasted vegetable frittata

1 small zucchini, diced

1 red bell pepper, diced

1 yellow bell pepper, diced

1 red onion, diced

⅓ cup olive oil

Kosher salt and freshly ground black pepper to taste

2 garlic cloves, minced

12 eggs

1 cup half & half

⅓ cup grated Parmesan cheese

1 tablespoon butter

⅓ cup chopped green onions

½ cup grated Gruyère cheese

Preheat oven to 425°. Place zucchini, peppers and onion on a baking sheet. Drizzle with olive oil and sprinkle with salt and pepper. Toss well. Bake for 15 minutes, add garlic, toss with a spatula and bake for another 15 minutes. When vegetables are cooked, remove from the oven and reduce heat to 350°.

Beat the eggs with a whisk; add half & half, Parmesan cheese, salt and pepper. Combine well.

In 14-inch ovenproof skillet, heat butter and sauté green onions over medium-low heat for 1 minute. Add the roasted vegetables to the skillet and toss with the green onions. Pour egg mixture over vegetables and cook for 2 minutes over medium-low heat.

Bake the frittata for 20 to 30 minutes, until puffed and set in the middle. Sprinkle with the Gruyère and bake for another 3 minutes, until the cheese is melted. Cut into 8 wedges and serve hot or at room temperature.

tuscan scrambled eggs

6 tablespoons butter, divided

1¼ cups sliced mushrooms

¼ pound prosciutto or ham, diced or slivered

¾ teaspoon minced garlic

½ medium green bell pepper, diced

½ pound asparagus or broccoli, trimmed and cut into 1-inch pieces

10 eggs

1½ tablespoons fresh minced basil or 1¼ teaspoons dried basil

1 teaspoon dried oregano

¼ teaspoon kosher salt

¾ teaspoon freshly ground black pepper

¼ teaspoon crushed red pepper flakes

6 ounces cream cheese

1½ cups shredded mozzarella cheese

⅓ cup grated Parmesan cheese

In a 14-inch skillet, melt 2 tablespoons butter; add mushrooms, prosciutto, garlic and green pepper. Sauté over medium heat until vegetables are tender. Remove with a slotted spoon and set aside.

Blanch asparagus or broccoli in boiling salted water for 1 to 2 minutes until crisp-tender; drain and cool in ice water. Drain well and set aside.

Whisk together eggs, basil, oregano, salt, black pepper and red pepper flakes. Cut cream cheese into bits and add to egg mixture. Heat remaining 4 tablespoons butter in skillet; add egg mixture. Cook over medium heat while folding mixture with a spatula to blend in cream cheese. When eggs are half set, add warm vegetable-prosciutto mixture, mozzarella, Parmesan and warm asparagus or broccoli. Continue to cook while gently folding in cheese with a spatula. When eggs are just done, serve immediately.

sunrise cheese soufflé

3 tablespoons butter

3 tablespoons all-purpose flour

¾ cup milk

4 egg yolks, slightly beaten, room temperature

¾ teaspoon kosher salt

1 teaspoon dry mustard

Dash of hot pepper sauce

1½ cups grated Cheddar cheese

5 egg whites, room temperature

Grated Parmesan cheese

Preheat oven to 375°. Melt the butter in a heavy saucepan and blend in the flour over medium heat, stirring 2 to 3 minutes. Stir in the milk, whisking until thickened. Remove from the heat and slowly stir in the yolks. (If it is too hot, eggs will scramble.) Add salt, dry mustard, hot pepper sauce and cheese. Stir to incorporate.

Let the yolk mixture stand while you beat the egg whites stiffly but not dry. Fold some of the egg whites into the cheese mixture fairly thoroughly and add the remainder more lightly.

Pour into a buttered 6-cup soufflé dish and smooth the top. Sprinkle with grated Parmesan cheese. Bake for 30 to 35 minutes or until the mixture is well risen and delicately brown. Serve immediately before it falls.

fiesta sweet corn and bacon quiche

Cornmeal Crust

1 cup all-purpose flour

¼ cup yellow cornmeal

¼ teaspoon kosher salt

2 tablespoons grated Parmesan cheese

6 tablespoons butter, cold, cut into pieces

1 egg

CHEF TIP:

THE CORNMEAL CRUST ADDS
A SPECIAL CRUNCH TO THIS
QUICHE.

Filling

6 slices bacon, cooked until crisp, broken into ½-inch pieces

2 ears corn, kernels cut from cobs (1½ to 2 cups corn) or
    1 (15.25-ounce) can corn kernels seasoned with red and green
    chiles, drained

1 (4.5-ounce) can chopped green chiles, drained

1 (4.25-ounce) can sliced ripe olives, drained

1 cup grated Monterey Jack cheese

5 eggs

1½ cups half & half

½ teaspoon kosher salt

Pinch of cayenne pepper

To make the crust, in the bowl of a food processor, combine the flour, cornmeal, salt and Parmesan cheese. Add the butter and pulse until the mixture is crumbly and like coarse meal. Beat egg; gradually add to flour mixture, pulsing until it is evenly moistened and begins to cling together. Remove from the bowl and shape into a flattened ball. On a floured counter, roll out the dough to a 13-inch circle. Fit the pastry into a 10-inch quiche dish or deep pie plate; press edge under, even with top of dish.

Preheat oven to 450°. To prepare the filling, evenly distribute bacon, corn, chiles, olives and Jack cheese in the crust. Beat eggs with half & half, salt and pepper. Pour egg mixture over the top.

Bake quiche for 10 minutes; reduce heat to 350° and continue baking until filling is nicely browned and set in center, 20 to 25 minutes longer. If crust gets too brown before the filling is set, cover it loosely with foil.

Remove from the oven and let stand for 10 minutes. Cut into wedges and serve.

sunshine pancake with fresh berries

2½ tablespoons butter

1¼ cups milk

¾ cup all-purpose flour

3 eggs

⅓ cup sugar

¼ teaspoon kosher salt

¼ teaspoon pure vanilla extract

Powdered sugar

Fresh berries (raspberries, strawberries or blueberries)

Maple syrup, heated

Preheat oven to 400°. Place butter in a 9-inch glass pie plate and melt in the oven. In a blender or the bowl of a food processor, combine milk, flour, eggs, sugar, salt and vanilla; process until smooth.

Remove pie plate from oven and increase temperature to 425°. Pour batter into pie plate and return to oven. Bake 20 minutes. Reduce oven temperature to 325° and bake 8 to 10 minutes longer. Invert on serving platter. Sprinkle with powdered sugar and serve with fresh berries and warm maple syrup.

crème brûlée french toast

½ cup butter

1 cup packed brown sugar

2 tablespoons light corn syrup

1 (8 to 9-inch) round loaf country-style bread

5 eggs

1½ cups half & half

1 teaspoon pure vanilla extract

1 teaspoon orange-flavored liqueur

¼ teaspoon kosher salt

In a small heavy saucepan, melt butter with brown sugar and corn syrup over moderate heat, stirring until smooth. Pour into a 9 x 13 x 2-inch baking dish. Cut 6, 1-inch thick slices from center portion of bread, reserving ends for another use, and trim crusts. Arrange bread slices in one layer in baking dish, squeezing them slightly to fit.

In a bowl, whisk together eggs, half & half, vanilla, liqueur and salt until combined well; pour evenly over bread. Chill bread mixture, covered, at least 8 hours and up to 1 day. Bring to room temperature before baking.

Preheat oven to 350°. Bake, uncovered, in middle of oven until puffed and edges are pale golden, 35 to 40 minutes. Serve hot.

orange blossom butter

1 cup butter, room temperature

½ cup honey

6 tablespoons orange juice, room temperature

1 tablespoon grated orange zest

Combine butter, honey, juice and zest; blend well.

upside-down sausage and apple cornbread

Sausage and Apples

½ pound small pork sausage links

4 tablespoons butter

½ cup packed light brown sugar

4 apples, peeled, cored and cut into eighths

Cornbread

1 cup all-purpose flour

¾ cup yellow cornmeal

3 tablespoons packed light brown sugar

1 tablespoon baking powder

1 teaspoon kosher salt

1 egg, lightly beaten

4 tablespoons butter

1 cup milk

Maple syrup, heated, for serving

VARIATION:
1 (7.5 OUNCE) BOX OF
YELLOW CORN MUFFIN MIX
CAN BE SUBSTITUTED FOR THE
CORN BREAD RECIPE. MAKE
ACCORDING TO PACKAGE
DIRECTIONS.

To prepare the sausage and apples, oil the bottom and sides of an 8 x 8 x 2-inch square pan. Brown the sausages in a medium skillet over moderately high heat, rotating them until browned and cooked through. Remove the sausages and discard all but 2 tablespoons drippings. Add the butter and brown sugar to the skillet. Heat, stirring, until the sugar is melted. Add the apples and sauté them over moderate heat, turning occasionally, until soft, about 10 minutes.

Arrange the sausages in rows across the bottom of the prepared pan. Insert the apple slices, rounded-sides down, between the rows of sausage, wedging them in tightly. Pour pan juices over sausages. The pan can be covered and refrigerated overnight at this point.

Preheat oven to 400°. To make the cornbread, stir the flour, cornmeal, brown sugar, baking powder and salt in a medium bowl. Add the egg, melted butter and milk, and stir with a wooden spoon until well combined. Pour the batter over the apples and sausages, smoothing the top to cover well. Bake for 20 to 25 minutes, or until a cake tester inserted into the bread comes out clean. Remove from the oven and immediately invert onto a platter. Serve in squares with maple syrup.

maple-glazed bacon

1 pound thickly sliced bacon

½ cup maple syrup

1 teaspoon dry mustard

Preheat oven to 400°. Line a shallow-rimmed baking sheet or broiler pan with heavy foil. Place a rack in the pan and arrange the bacon on the rack. Whisk the maple syrup and mustard together in a small bowl. Brush mixture over the top of the bacon. Bake for 15 minutes. Turn the bacon over and brush again with syrup mixture. Bake an additional 5 to 10 minutes, or until the bacon is very crisp and golden. Remove the pan from the oven and let the bacon rest on the rack for 5 minutes, then loosen. Do not drain on paper towels as the bacon will stick.

The bacon can be wrapped in foil and refrigerated or frozen. Reheat on the rack at 400° for 5 minutes.

During the mid-1920's, the potential for a social winter haven in Boca Grande was discovered by Louise (DuPont) and Frank Crowninshield. Besides building a lovely house and bringing their friends to visit, Louise became the adored patroness—the "Godmother"—of the island, founding a school and a health clinic. Several generations later, the DuPont family still wields a positive influence on the island. The Gasparilla Inn and Club, the pulse of Boca Grande, is owned by Sarah and Will Farish—she, the daughter of Bayard Sharp, a DuPont cousin and longtime, visionary owner of the Inn, and he, a former U.S. Ambassador to Britain's Court of St. James's. Every television set in Boca Grande tuned in to watch the Farishes entertaining their good friends Queen Elizabeth II and Prince Philip at the Kentucky Derby in 2006.

mini magic biscuits

Makes 24 mini biscuits

1 cup sour cream

½ cup melted butter

2 cups biscuit baking mix

Preheat oven to 400°. Mix together sour cream, butter and biscuit baking mix. Put mixture in miniature muffin tins that have been well oiled. Bake for 15 minutes or until golden.

NOTE:

A FAVORITE RECIPE FROM

BOCA GRANDE ENTERTAINS.

perfect cream biscuits

Makes 12 biscuits

2 cups all-purpose flour

1 teaspoon kosher salt

1 tablespoon baking powder

2 teaspoons sugar

1 to 1½ cups heavy cream

⅓ cup melted butter

Preheat oven to 425°. Combine the flour, salt, baking powder and sugar in a mixing bowl. Stir the dry ingredients with a fork to blend and lighten. Slowly add 1 cup of the cream to the mixture, stirring constantly. Gather the dough together; when it holds together and feels tender it is ready to knead. Add more cream if necessary.

Place the dough on a lightly floured board and knead for 1 minute. Pat or roll the dough into a square that is ¹/₂-inch thick. Cut into 12 squares and dip each square into the melted butter so that all sides are coated. Place biscuits 2-inches apart on a baking sheet. Bake 15 minutes, or until the biscuits are lightly browned. Serve hot.

gasparilla granola

4 cups regular oats (not instant or quick-cooking)

⅔ cup wheat germ

⅔ cup unsweetened large flake coconut

6 tablespoons sesame seeds

6 tablespoons sunflower seeds

½ cup raw cashews, or sliced almonds, or both

⅔ cup canola oil

⅓ cup honey

¼ cup brown sugar

1 teaspoon pure vanilla extract

¼ teaspoon kosher salt

½ cup dried cranberries, or other dried fruit

CHEF TIP:

GRANOLA INGREDIENTS CAN BE PURCHASED IN BULK AT A HEALTH FOOD STORE.

Preheat oven to 300°. Mix together oats, wheat germ, coconut, sesame seeds, sunflower seeds and nuts in a large bowl.

In a saucepan, combine oil, honey, brown sugar, vanilla and salt. Cook over low heat until honey is melted. Pour over the dry mixture and blend thoroughly. Spread on a lightly oiled 10 x 15 x 1-inch baking sheet and bake for 35 to 40 minutes, stirring every 10 minutes. Cool thoroughly; add dried fruit and store in a zip-top plastic bag or airtight container. Serve with fresh fruit and milk.

blueberry morning cake

Topping

½ cup sugar

¼ cup all-purpose flour

½ teaspoon cinnamon

4 tablespoons butter, chilled and cut into bits

Cake

2 cups all-purpose flour

2 teaspoons baking powder

½ teaspoon kosher salt

4 tablespoons butter, room temperature

¾ cup sugar

1 egg

½ cup milk

1 pint fresh blueberries

To prepare topping, combine sugar, flour and cinnamon. Cut in butter until mixture resembles coarse meal and set aside.

Preheat oven to 375°. Butter an 8-inch square baking pan; dust with flour. Sift together flour, baking powder and salt. With electric mixer, cream butter and sugar until light and fluffy. Beat in egg and milk. Add flour mixture in batches, beating until just combined. Fold in blueberries; pour batter into baking pan. Sprinkle topping evenly over batter. Bake 35 to 45 minutes or until cake tester comes out clean.

rhubarb sweet bread

1 teaspoon baking soda

1 cup buttermilk

1½ cups packed light brown sugar

⅔ cup canola oil

1 egg, beaten

1 teaspoon pure vanilla extract

1 teaspoon kosher salt

2½ cups all-purpose flour

1½ cups fresh or frozen rhubarb (defrosted), cut into 1-inch pieces

½ cup chopped walnuts or pecans

½ cup sugar

1 tablespoon butter, room temperature

Preheat oven to 325°. Butter and lightly flour two 4 x 9-inch loaf pans. In a small bowl, dissolve the baking soda in the buttermilk.

Combine the brown sugar, oil, egg, vanilla and salt in a large bowl and mix well. Stir in the buttermilk mixture. Add the flour gradually and stir just until moistened. Fold in the rhubarb and nuts. Divide the batter into buttered loaf pans.

Mix the sugar and butter in a bowl until crumbly. Sprinkle the crumb mixture over the batter. Bake 50 to 55 minutes or until cake tester inserted in the center comes out clean. Cool in the pans on a wire rack for 10 minutes. Remove the loaves from the pans and cool on a wire rack. Serve with whipped butter or vanilla ice cream, if desired.

lemon ribbon bread

Bread Batter

½ cup butter, room temperature

1 cup sugar

1 egg

2 teaspoons grated lemon zest

1½ cups all-purpose flour

1 teaspoon baking powder

½ teaspoon kosher salt

1 cup chopped pecans or walnuts

½ cup milk

Filling

6 ounces cream cheese, room temperature

⅓ cup sugar

1 tablespoon flour

1 egg

Powdered sugar

Preheat oven to 350°. Butter a 4 x 9-inch loaf pan. To prepare bread batter, in a large bowl, cream butter, sugar, egg and lemon zest. In another bowl, mix flour, baking powder, salt and nuts. Add to creamed mixture alternately with milk, beating until smooth after each addition. Set aside.

For filling, combine cream cheese, sugar, flour and egg. Beat until smooth. Spread one half of the bread batter into the loaf pan. Top with filling. Spoon remaining half of bread batter evenly over filling. Bake 60 minutes or until top springs back when touched lightly. Sprinkle with powdered sugar while warm.

raspberry-sour cream muffins

Topping

½ cup light brown sugar

⅓ cup all-purpose flour

1 teaspoon cinnamon

2 tablespoons butter, room temperature

Muffins

1½ cups plus 1 tablespoon all-purpose flour

2 teaspoons baking powder

¼ teaspoon baking soda

½ teaspoon kosher salt

1 egg

¾ cup sugar

1 tablespoon butter, melted

1 cup sour cream

1 teaspoon pure vanilla extract

¾ teaspoon finely grated lemon zest

1 cup raspberries or blueberries

For the topping, combine brown sugar, flour and cinnamon. Add butter and rub with fingers to form coarse crumbs. Refrigerate until ready to use.

Preheat oven to 375°. Butter a 12-cup muffin pan. To prepare batter, in a medium bowl, whisk the 1½ cups of flour with the baking powder, baking soda and salt.

In a large bowl, using a mixer, beat the egg until frothy. Add the sugar and melted butter and beat until pale yellow. Beat in the sour cream, vanilla and lemon zest until blended.

Add the dry ingredients and beat at low speed until just combined.

In a bowl, toss the berries with the remaining 1 tablespoon of flour. Using a rubber spatula, fold the berries into the batter. Fill the muffin cups three-fourths full of batter and sprinkle with the topping. Bake for 25 minutes, or until a cake tester inserted in the center of a muffin comes out clean. Remove the muffins from the pan and let cool on a rack.

crusty baguettes

Makes 4 loaves

3 cups very warm water (105 to 115 degrees)

1 tablespoon dry yeast

1 tablespoon sugar

7 cups all-purpose flour

1 tablespoon kosher salt

Oil well 2 double baguette pans. Combine the water, yeast and sugar in a large bowl (1 gallon capacity or more) and allow the yeast to "proof" for a few minutes. Add the flour and salt. Mix thoroughly with a spoon; do not knead. Cover the bowl tightly with plastic wrap and set in a warm place. Allow dough to rise at least 2 to 3 hours or until it has doubled.

When you are ready to bake, turn out the dough onto a heavily floured board or counter; it will be sticky. Divide it in four with a sharp knife. Shape each piece into a free form loaf about 4-inches shorter than the baguette pans. Place loaves in pans. Cover lightly and set aside in a warm place until nearly doubled.

While the bread is rising, preheat oven to 425°. When ready to bake, place pans on middle shelf. Bake bread for 20 minutes or until crusty and brown. Cool uncovered on a wire rack. Can be warmed before serving at 350° for 5 to 10 minutes.

VARIATION:

SUBSTITUTE WHOLE WHEAT FLOUR, WHEAT GERM, CORNMEAL OR SEMOLINA FOR PART OF THE WHITE FLOUR. EXPERIMENT FREELY TO GET THE TASTE AND TEXTURE YOU LIKE BUT ALWAYS USE MORE THAN HALF WHITE UNBLEACHED FLOUR WHEN MAKING BREAD. IT HAS MORE GLUTEN AND WILL HELP THE BREAD RISE. ADD 2 TO 4 TABLESPOONS CHOPPED ROSEMARY, BASIL, CHIVES OR YOUR FAVORITE HERB WITH THE FLOUR AND SALT.

NOTE:

A FAVORITE RECIPE FROM BOCA GRANDE ENTERTAINS.

alsatian cheese tart

1 sheet frozen puff pastry, thawed in refrigerator

⅓ cup whole-milk cottage cheese

3 tablespoons sour cream

Kosher salt and freshly ground black pepper to taste

4 slices bacon, cooked and crumbled, 2 tablespoons of drippings
      reserved

⅓ cup thinly sliced onion

2 tablespoons grated Parmesan cheese

NOTE:

THIS TART IS A DELICIOUS
ACCOMPANIMENT TO EGG
DISHES, SALADS OR SOUPS.

Preheat oven to 400°. Place puff pastry on a lightly floured surface
and roll to increase size slightly. Remove to a baking sheet.

In a blender, combine cottage cheese, sour cream, salt and
pepper; blend until smooth.

In the reserved drippings, sauté the onion until soft. Spread cottage
cheese mixture over top of pastry; sprinkle bacon, onion and
Parmesan cheese over top. Bake for 10 to 12 minutes, or until
golden.

mango smoothie

3 mangoes

8 ounces vanilla yogurt

1 banana

2 cups fresh orange juice

Juice of 1 lime

1 cup crushed ice

Pinch of salt

2 tablespoons protein powder (optional)

Combine the mangoes, yogurt, banana, orange juice, lime juice,
ice, salt and protein powder in a blender. Process on high for at least
3 minutes or until very smooth.

cheesy onion bread

Makes 1 loaf

¾ cup butter, cold, divided

1 finely chopped onion

1 tablespoon poppy seeds

Kosher salt and freshly ground black pepper to taste

1 cup coarsely shredded Gruyère cheese (3-ounces)

2 cups all-purpose flour

2 teaspoons baking powder

½ teaspoon baking soda

1 teaspoon kosher salt

1 cup buttermilk

CHEF TIP:

ALWAYS COOK ONIONS ON LOW OR MEDIUM HEAT. HIGH HEAT MAKES THEM BITTER.

Preheat oven to 425°. Butter a 4 x 9-inch metal loaf pan. In a large skillet, melt 4 tablespoons butter; pour 2 tablespoons of the melted butter into a small bowl and reserve. Add the onion to the skillet and cook over medium heat, stirring occasionally, until it is softened, about 8 minutes. Stir in the poppy seeds and season with salt and pepper. Scrape the onion mixture onto a plate and refrigerate for 5 minutes, until cooled slightly. Stir in the Gruyère.

In the bowl of a food processor, pulse the flour with the baking powder, baking soda and salt. Cube remaining 8 tablespoons butter and add it to the flour mixture. Pulse until it is the size of small peas. Add the buttermilk and pulse 5 or 6 times, just until a soft dough forms.

Turn the dough out onto a well-floured work surface and knead 2 or 3 times. Pat or roll the dough into a 3-inch by 12 to 14-inch rectangle. Spread onion mixture on top of dough and press down lightly. Cut the dough crosswise into 10 pieces. Using a spatula, remove the dough pieces from the surface and stack them, one on top of the other, onion side up. This will create a tower of dough pieces. Carefully lay the stack in the prepared loaf pan and brush with the reserved butter. (The dough will spread to fill the pan.)

Bake the loaf in the center of the oven for about 30 minutes, until it has risen and is golden. Let the bread cool on a rack for at least 15 minutes before unmolding and serving.

Creating the stack of dough pieces and placing them in the pan can seem tricky at first but the dough is very forgiving. Your efforts will be rewarded.

gruyère shortbread

6 tablespoons butter, room temperature

½ teaspoon kosher salt

2 egg yolks

¼ teaspoon cayenne pepper

1 cup shredded Gruyère cheese

1 cup all-purpose flour

Preheat oven to 350°. Combine butter, salt, egg yolks, cayenne pepper and cheese in the bowl of a food processor by pulsing 6 times. Process for 6 seconds. Add flour and process until dough begins to come together. Pat dough into an 8 x 4-inch rectangle on a baking sheet. Cut rectangle in half. Cut each half into 4 triangles; separate triangles slightly with knife. Bake for 25 minutes or until golden. If necessary, separate triangles again while hot. Cool on baking sheet 3 minutes. Transfer to a rack and serve warm.

This shortbread is a tasty accompaniment to soups and salads.

grande oranges and strawberries

½ cup orange marmalade

1½ cups sparkling white grape juice, chilled

¼ cup orange liqueur

10 to 12 navel oranges, peeled and sectioned
   (cut between the membranes)

2 cups sliced fresh strawberries

GARNISH: **Fresh mint sprigs**

Melt marmalade in a small saucepan over low heat, stirring constantly. Remove from heat and cool slightly. Stir together marmalade, white grape juice and orange liqueur in a large serving dish until blended. Add orange sections and stir gently. Cover and chill 8 hours. Add strawberries and toss gently. Serve with slotted spoon and garnish with mint.

soups
& sandwiches

iced avocado soup

6 ripe avocados

5 cups chicken stock

2 cups light cream or half & half

4 to 6 tablespoons fresh lime juice

Dash of hot pepper sauce

Pinch of cayenne pepper

Kosher salt and freshly ground black pepper to taste

GARNISH: Thin slices of lime

   Chopped cilantro

Purée avocados with chicken stock in a blender. Combine with cream, lime juice, hot pepper sauce, cayenne, salt and pepper, blending well with a whisk. Chill.

Serve in ice-cold soup cups, garnished with lime slices and cilantro.

pea soup with mint

Serves 4 to 6

1 tablespoon butter

2 leeks, chopped, white part only

4 cups chicken stock

1 (20-ounce) package frozen green peas

2 teaspoons fresh lemon juice

Kosher salt and freshly ground black pepper to taste

¾ cup heavy cream

2 tablespoons chopped fresh mint or to taste

GARNISH: Mint sprigs

NOTE:

THE LEEK, NATIVE TO THE MEDITERRANEAN, LOOKS LIKE A GIANT GREEN ONION BUT ITS FLAVOR AND FRAGRANCE ARE MILDER AND MORE SUBTLE. THE SMALLER THE LEEK, THE MORE TENDER IT WILL BE. BEFORE COOKING LEEKS, SLIT THEM FROM TOP TO BOTTOM AND WASH THOROUGHLY UNDER RUNNING WARM WATER TO REMOVE ALL THE DIRT TRAPPED BETWEEN THE LEAF LAYERS.

In a saucepan, melt butter and sauté leeks until translucent. Add stock, peas, lemon juice, salt and pepper. Bring to a boil and simmer for 1 to 2 minutes, stirring frequently. Purée in a food processor or blender until smooth. Stir in cream and chopped mint; chill.

Serve garnished with mint.

chilled cucumber and shrimp soup

2 large cucumbers, peeled, seeded and coarsely chopped

¼ cup red wine vinegar

1 tablespoon sugar

1 teaspoon kosher salt

1 pound medium shrimp, uncooked, peeled and deveined

2 tablespoons butter

¼ cup dry white vermouth

1 tablespoon fresh lemon juice

Kosher salt and freshly ground black pepper to taste

3 (7-ounce) containers Greek-style yogurt

1 cup half & half

⅓ cup chopped fresh dill

GARNISH: Sour cream

Fresh sprigs of dill

Toss cucumbers with vinegar, sugar and salt. Let stand 30 minutes.
Sauté shrimp in butter just until pink, 2 to 3 minutes. Remove shrimp
and reserve. Add vermouth and lemon juice to skillet and boil until
reduced to a few spoonfuls. Pour sauce over shrimp and season
with salt and pepper.

Drain cucumbers and process briefly in the bowl of a food processor.
Add yogurt and half & half; process until smooth. Combine soup
with dill, shrimp and sauce. Cover and refrigerate until very cold.
Serve in chilled bowls topped with a dollop of sour cream and a
small sprig of dill.

tomato soup with dill

2 medium onions, chopped

2 garlic cloves, chopped

1 tablespoon butter

2 pounds fresh tomatoes, chopped or 1 (26-ounce) can crushed
 tomatoes, with liquid

2 chicken or beef bouillon cubes

1½ tablespoons chopped fresh dill

2 tablespoons mayonnaise

2 cups buttermilk

Kosher salt and freshly ground black pepper to taste

GARNISH: Sour cream

 Fresh dill sprigs

Sauté onions and garlic in butter until onions are translucent. Add
tomatoes, bouillon cubes and dill. Cover and simmer for 10 minutes;
cool.

Purée mixture in blender until very smooth, in batches if necessary.
Add mayonnaise and blend until combined. Pour into bowl and
add buttermilk, salt and pepper to taste. Chill.

Serve topped with dollop of sour cream and fresh dill sprig.

turkish tomato soup

2 cups tomato-vegetable juice

1 cup tomato juice

1 cup sour cream or yogurt

1 tablespoon olive oil

1 tablespoon lemon juice

1½ tablespoons white wine vinegar

1 teaspoon curry powder

2 to 3 dashes hot pepper sauce

1 tablespoon chopped fresh mint

1 tablespoon chopped fresh basil

Kosher salt and freshly ground black pepper to taste

GARNISH: Chopped parsley

Chopped basil

Combine tomato-vegetable juice, tomato juice, sour cream, olive oil, lemon juice, wine vinegar, curry powder, hot pepper sauce, mint, basil, salt and pepper in a blender and blend until smooth. Chill 4 hours or more. Serve garnished with parsley and basil.

The Gasparilla Inn and Club, an aging Grande Dame dressed in pale yellow, trimmed in white with a touch of pink geraniums, sets an understated, elegant tone in Boca Grande. Sarah Farish is the Chairman of the Board and under her thoughtful leadership, the Inn has been transformed into its current regal stature, accompanied by impeccable service. If you are an Inn guest, you have all the privileges of membership: the Beach Club with its daily sumptuous luncheon buffet, verandas, swimming pools, a Spa with Fitness Center, tennis courts, croquet court, and a beautifully landscaped Pete Dye signature golf course. One of the favorite evening pastimes for families during Christmas and spring vacation at the Inn is bingo, which is held in the newly decorated wicker and chintz parlor. It is not unusual for a five-year-old to win a $100 pot. It's a great training ground for future Wall Streeters.

bayou baked clam soup

¾ pound medium potatoes, unpeeled

2 tablespoons butter

⅓ cup sliced green onions

1 garlic clove, minced

2 tablespoons flour

½ teaspoon dry mustard

¼ teaspoon celery seed

⅛ teaspoon cayenne pepper

1 cup milk

1 tablespoon white wine Worcestershire sauce

2 tablespoons freshly grated Parmesan cheese

1 cup shredded Swiss cheese, divided

4 (6.5-ounce) cans minced clams, drained (reserve juice of 3 cans)

1 cup cottage cheese

¼ cup chopped fresh parsley

GARNISH: Crumbled crisp bacon

In a large saucepan, cook unpeeled potatoes in salted water about 20 minutes or until tender; drain. Peel and cut into 1-inch cubes (about 4 cups). Set aside.

Butter a 1½ quart baking dish. In a medium saucepan, melt butter. Add green onions and garlic. Sauté 2 to 3 minutes until tender. Stir in flour, mustard, celery seed and cayenne pepper until smooth. Cook and stir 1 minute. Remove from heat and stir in milk. Return to heat, cook, while stirring for 3 to 5 minutes until sauce thickens. Reduce heat; stir in Worcestershire sauce, Parmesan cheese and ¾ cup Swiss cheese. Simmer 1 minute until cheeses are melted. Remove from heat.

Preheat oven to 350°. In a blender, combine reserved clam juice and cottage cheese. Process until smooth. Stir into cheese sauce. Fold in potatoes, clams and parsley. Spoon into baking dish. Sprinkle top with remaining ¼ cup Swiss cheese. Bake for 30 minutes until thoroughly heated and lightly browned. Serve garnished with crumbled bacon.

bay scallop and grouper cheek chowder with fennel

4 slices bacon, diced

1 large onion, diced

½ teaspoon kosher salt

½ teaspoon freshly ground black pepper

Pinch of fennel seeds

2 ribs celery, sliced

1 large fennel bulb, diced, fronds reserved

1 garlic clove, minced

1 bay leaf

1 pound potatoes, peeled and diced

4 cups chicken stock

1 (28-ounce) can plum tomatoes, undrained

1 (8-ounce) bottle clam juice

3 tablespoons licorice-flavored liqueur (optional)

1 pound bay scallops

¾ pound grouper cheeks or cubed, firm white fish

GARNISH: Oyster crackers (optional)

NOTE:

GROUPER, A MEMBER OF THE SEA BASS FAMILY, IS FOUND IN THE WATERS OF THE GULF OF MEXICO. IT HAS A FIRM, LEAN FLESH SUITABLE FOR BROILING, BAKING OR FRYING. SAUTÉED MORSELS OF GROUPER CHEEKS ARE A SPECIAL TREAT.

In a soup pot, cook bacon until golden for 3 minutes. Add onion, salt, pepper and fennel seeds and cook, stirring, until onion is limp, about 5 minutes. Stir in the celery, fennel, garlic and bay leaf; sauté for 10 minutes. Add potatoes, stock, tomatoes and clam juice. Bring to a simmer and cook for 20 minutes. Add liqueur and simmer for 10 minutes.

Chop fennel fronds to yield 2 or 3 tablespoons. Add to pot along with bay scallops and grouper cheeks. Simmer gently just until seafood is cooked through. Serve with oyster crackers, if desired.

boca gumbo

1 pound andouille sausage, diced into small pieces

½ cup canola oil

½ cup flour

1 large red onion, chopped fine

6 celery ribs, chopped fine

2 carrots, chopped fine

¼ cup Cajun seasoning

8 cups chicken stock

6 cups clam juice

4 ounces tomato paste

1 pound crayfish, tails only

1 pound medium shrimp, peeled and deveined

Kosher salt and freshly ground black pepper to taste

In a large, heavy bottomed pot, sauté sausage until lightly browned. Remove with a slotted spoon and set aside.

Add oil to the pot and heat over medium-high heat until almost smoking. Add flour and stir constantly until the roux turns a deep brown (about the color of peanut butter), 10 to 12 minutes. Add onion, celery, carrots and Cajun seasoning and cook, stirring, for 5 minutes. Slowly whisk in the chicken stock and clam juice; add tomato paste and whisk to combine. Simmer for about 15 minutes until thickened.

Add crayfish tails, shrimp, and reserved sausage. Bring to a boil, reduce heat and simmer for 5 minutes, until crayfish and shrimp are done. Adjust seasoning.

This gumbo is best made one day ahead and refrigerated. To serve, bring to a simmer slowly.

gulf chowder

3 strips bacon

3 carrots, sliced

3 celery ribs, sliced

1 green bell pepper, chopped

2 garlic cloves, minced

1 (32-ounce) bottle tomato-clam juice

1 cup white wine

1 (10-ounce) can diced tomatoes with green chiles

1 bay leaf

1 teaspoon seafood seasoning

6 peppercorns, cracked

1 teaspoon cayenne pepper

Kosher salt to taste

1 pound grouper cheeks or cubed, firm white fish

1 pound medium shrimp, peeled and deveined

2 pounds mussels, beards removed and mussels scrubbed

Cooked pasta or rice

VARIATION:

OKRA AND/OR CORN CAN BE
ADDED TO THIS CHOWDER.

In a skillet, fry bacon. Remove and drain on paper towels and crumble. To the drippings in the skillet, add carrots, celery, green bell pepper and garlic; sauté for 5 minutes. Transfer to crockpot and add juice, wine, tomatoes, bay leaf, seafood seasoning, peppercorns, cayenne, salt and the reserved bacon. Cook on low heat for 8 hours. As an alternative, tomato-vegetable stock can be simmered on stovetop for 1 hour.

To serve the same day, add fish, shrimp and mussels; simmer 5 minutes or until mussels open. Discard any mussels that do not open. Serve over pasta or rice.

Tomato-vegetable stock, without fish and shellfish, can be refrigerated overnight, reheated, adding and cooking the fish and shellfish briefly.

poblano corn chowder with shrimp

4 tablespoons butter, divided, room temperature

2 tablespoons flour

1 medium onion, chopped

3 celery ribs, chopped

2 large poblano chiles, seeded and chopped

2 (15-ounce) cans cream-style corn

1 (16-ounce) package frozen corn kernels, thawed

2 (14-ounce) cans low-sodium chicken stock

1 cup fat-free half & half, mixed with 1 teaspoon cornstarch

2 teaspoons sugar

½ teaspoon cayenne pepper

1 pound uncooked medium shrimp, peeled, deveined, and coarsely chopped

4 tablespoons chopped fresh cilantro

Kosher salt and freshly ground black pepper to taste

GARNISH: Chopped fresh cilantro

Blend 2 tablespoons butter and flour in a small bowl; set aside. Melt remaining 2 tablespoons butter in a large pot over medium-high heat. Add onion, celery and chiles. Sauté until soft, about 6 minutes. Add creamed corn, corn kernels, stock, half & half mixture, sugar and cayenne; whisk in the butter-flour mixture. Simmer 15 minutes to blend flavors.

Add shrimp and cilantro. Simmer until shrimp are cooked through, about 5 minutes longer. Season with salt and pepper. Garnish with cilantro.

red bean and rice soup with shrimp

1 tablespoon canola oil

1 cup chopped onion

½ cup chopped celery

1 garlic clove, minced

2 tablespoons flour

1½ cups water

¼ cup long-grain rice, uncooked

1 teaspoon chili powder

½ teaspoon ground cumin

¼ teaspoon kosher salt

1 (14.5-ounce) can diced tomatoes, undrained

1 (10.5-ounce) can low-sodium chicken stock

1 pound medium shrimp, peeled and deveined

1 (15.5-ounce) can red kidney beans, drained

Lime wedges

Hot pepper sauce

Heat oil in a large Dutch oven over medium heat. Add onion, celery
and garlic; sauté 5 minutes. Sprinkle with flour; stir well and cook an
additional minute. Add 1½ cups water, rice, chili powder, cumin,
salt, tomatoes and chicken stock. Bring to a boil. Cover, reduce
heat and simmer 20 minutes. Adjust seasoning. Add shrimp and red
beans; stir well. Cook, uncovered, 3 minutes or until shrimp is cooked.
Serve with lime wedges and hot pepper sauce.

spicy carrot soup with red curry

1 tablespoon canola oil

4 carrots, thickly sliced

2 thin slices fresh ginger

1 onion, finely chopped

4 cups chicken stock

2 cups water

½ cup unsweetened coconut milk

½ teaspoon red curry paste or to taste

3 carrots, julienned

Kosher salt and freshly ground black pepper to taste

GARNISH: Unsweetened coconut milk, warmed

   Julienned green onions

   Chopped fresh cilantro

   Minced candied ginger

VARIATION:

CHOPPED COOKED CHICKEN BREAST OR CHOPPED STEAMED SHRIMP CAN BE ADDED TO THIS SOUP. FOR A VEGETARIAN DISH, PREPARE WITH TOFU AND VEGETABLE STOCK.

Heat the canola oil in a large saucepan. Stir in the sliced carrots and ginger. Cook over medium-high heat, stirring constantly, for 6 to 8 minutes, or until the carrots are tender-crisp and light brown. Add the onions and mix well. Cook for 2 minutes or until the onion is tender, stirring constantly. Stir in the stock, water, ½ cup coconut milk and curry paste. Bring to a simmer, cover, and cook for 25 minutes or until the carrots are tender.

Strain the liquid into another saucepan, reserving the solids. Discard the ginger. Transfer the solids to a blender. Add 2 cups of the reserved liquid to the blender and process until puréed. Return the purée to the saucepan and stir in the julienned carrots. Simmer for 5 minutes or until the carrots are tender, stirring occasionally. Season with salt and pepper.

To garnish, swirl one teaspoon of the coconut milk into each serving and sprinkle with julienned green onion, chopped cilantro and minced candied ginger.

roasted chicken with wild rice soup

1 (6-ounce) box long-grain and wild rice mix

1 tablespoon olive oil

1½ cups chopped red onion

2 cups chopped celery

1 cup chopped carrot

2 garlic cloves, chopped

8 ounces mushrooms, halved

¼ cup flour

½ teaspoon dried tarragon

¼ teaspoon dried thyme

2 cups water

2 tablespoons dry sherry

4 cups chicken stock

1 (12-ounce) can fat-free evaporated milk

3 cups rotisserie chicken, chopped

Prepare rice according to package directions; set aside.

Heat oil in a large Dutch oven over medium-high heat. Add chopped onion, celery, carrot, garlic and mushrooms. Sauté for 6 minutes or until onion is tender. Stir the flour, tarragon and thyme into the onion mixture and cook for 1 minute, stirring frequently. Add water, sherry, chicken stock and evaporated milk; bring the mixture to a boil. Reduce heat and simmer for 20 minutes or until slightly thick. Stir in cooked rice and chicken. Cook for 10 minutes or until thoroughly heated.

south-of-the-border chicken soup

2 tablespoons olive oil

2 bunches green onions, chopped

1 teaspoon ground cumin

1½ teaspoons paprika

4 cups low-sodium chicken stock

1 (14-ounce) can stewed tomatoes, undrained

3 cups rotisserie chicken, chopped

3 teaspoons hot pepper sauce

2 (15-ounce) cans hominy, undrained

⅔ cup chopped fresh cilantro

1 (4-ounce) can chopped green chiles (optional)

GARNISH: Low-fat sour cream

Crumbled tortilla chips

NOTE:

HOMINY IS ONE OF THE FIRST FOOD GIFTS THE AMERICAN INDIANS GAVE TO THE COLONISTS. IT IS DRIED WHITE OR YELLOW CORN KERNELS FROM WHICH THE HULL AND GERM HAVE BEEN REMOVED. WHEN IT IS GROUND, IT IS CALLED HOMINY GRITS.

Heat oil in heavy pot over medium high heat. Add green onions, cumin and paprika. Sauté 3 to 5 minutes. Add stock, tomatoes, chicken and hot pepper sauce.

Purée hominy with its liquid in the bowl of a food processor or blender, in batches if necessary. Mix puréed hominy and green chilies (optional) into soup and bring to a boil. Reduce heat and simmer 15 minutes. Stir in cilantro.

Serve topped with a dollop of sour cream and crumbled tortilla chips.

lentil stew

4 tablespoons butter

1 (14-ounce) smoked kielbasa sausage, sliced

1 large onion, chopped

1½ cups lentils (French green lentils are best)

1 (14.5-ounce) can whole tomatoes, undrained and coarsely
   chopped

4 cups beef stock, divided

½ cup red wine

1 bay leaf

White rice, cooked

In a heavy pot, melt butter and sauté sliced sausage and onion until
onions are translucent and sausage is brown. Add lentils, tomatoes,
2 cups of beef stock, red wine and bay leaf. Simmer about 1 hour,
adding more beef stock as needed. Continue to simmer until the soup
is stew-like and the lentils are tender. Refrigerate for 24 hours before
serving. To serve, heat stew and ladle over prepared white rice.

Chopped fresh spinach can be added to this recipe.

It is hard to get lost in Boca Grande. There is one main street with no traffic lights from

the tollbooth at one end of the island to the lighthouse park at the other.

On the north end, there are clusters of condominiums, none higher than three stories,

which immediately separate the island from the high-rise communities in the

rest of Florida. There are several bridges to cross as one travels south, opening up the

view to the intercoastal waterway on the east and the expanse of Caribbean

blue Gulf waters to the west. It is impossible to drive onto the island without breathing

a sigh of relief. The clutter and clang of city life are left behind.

grande mushroom and green onion soup

½ cup butter

4 bunches green onions, coarsely chopped

½ teaspoon kosher salt

½ teaspoon white pepper

⅛ teaspoon cayenne pepper

3 tablespoons flour

6 cups chicken stock

1 pound white button mushrooms, cleaned and trimmed, divided

GARNISH: Sour cream

Thinly sliced green onion

Melt the butter in a medium soup pot until foaming. Add the green onions, salt, white pepper and cayenne pepper. Reduce the heat to low, cover and cook for 10 minutes, stirring occasionally. Do not brown. Remove the pan from the heat and stir in the flour; stir over low heat for 2 minutes. Add the chicken stock and whisk over moderately high heat until the soup comes to a boil. Reduce the heat to low and simmer, uncovered, for 10 minutes, stirring occasionally. Chop ¾ pound mushrooms (reserve the remaining ¼ pound to slice later). Add the chopped mushrooms to the soup and heat 1 minute. Purée the soup in batches in a blender or food processor fitted with the metal blade. Soup can be covered and refrigerated overnight or frozen.

To serve, slowly reheat the soup and adjust the seasonings. Slice the remaining ¼ pound of mushrooms and add to the soup. Simmer until they are soft.

Garnish each serving with a dollop of sour cream and a sprinkling of green onion.

pumpkin and apple soup

Serves 4 to 6

1 onion, chopped

3 garlic cloves, chopped

1 tablespoon butter, melted

3 cups chicken stock

1 (16-ounce) can pumpkin

1 to 2 tablespoons sugar

¼ teaspoon cinnamon

2 tart apples, peeled, cored and chopped

1 cup whipping cream or half & half

Kosher salt and freshly ground black pepper to taste

In a sauce pan, sauté onion and garlic in butter until onion is translucent. Add the stock, pumpkin, sugar, cinnamon and apples. Simmer until the apples are cooked and the flavors are blended. Purée in a blender. Return soup to saucepan and add cream, salt and pepper. Serve hot or at room temperature.

tangy turkey-brie panini

Serves 8

15 ounces Brie

16 multigrain or sourdough bread slices

2 pounds thinly sliced smoked turkey

½ cup red pepper jelly

2 tablespoons melted butter

Trim and discard rind from Brie. Cut Brie into ¹/₂-inch slices. Layer 8 bread slices evenly with turkey and Brie. Spread 1 tablespoon pepper jelly on one side of each of the remaining 8 bread slices. Place, jelly side down, onto Brie. Brush sandwiches with melted butter. Cook sandwiches, in batches, in a preheated panini press or in a large skillet until golden brown and cheese has melted.

hot and crusty shrimp sandwich

Marinade and Shrimp

2 tablespoons canola oil

1 garlic clove, minced

2 teaspoons dry mustard

1 teaspoon kosher salt

¼ cup fresh lemon juice

2 teaspoons red wine vinegar

Dash of cayenne pepper

½ red onion, thinly sliced

½ pound large raw shrimp, peeled and deveined

Sandwich

1 loaf (1 pound) French bread, cut in half horizontally (reserve top half for another use)

6 tablespoons butter, room temperature, divided

5 tablespoons chopped fresh parsley, divided

4 garlic cloves, minced

3 tablespoons sliced black olives

3 tablespoons chopped pimiento

To make the marinade, whisk together oil, garlic, mustard, salt, lemon juice, vinegar and cayenne in a medium glass bowl. Stir in the sliced onion and shrimp. Cover and marinate in the refrigerator 2 to 3 hours.

Preheat the oven to 400°. Remove as much bread as possible from the inside of the bottom half of the French bread, leaving a one-inch rim. Place the removed bread in the bowl of a food processor fitted with the metal blade; process into crumbs. Measure one cup of the crumbs and sauté them in 2 tablespoons of the butter until golden; set aside.

With a fork, mix the remaining 4 tablespoons butter with 3 tablespoons of the parsley and garlic in a small bowl. Spread the butter mixture on the bottom and side edges of the hollowed loaf. With a slotted spoon, remove the shrimp and onions from the marinade and place in the loaf. Sprinkle with the olives and pimiento. Drizzle with 3 tablespoons of the marinade. Discard remaining marinade. Sprinkle with the sautéed breadcrumbs and remaining 2 tablespoons parsley. Place the bread on a baking sheet and bake in the center of the oven for 18 to 20 minutes. Serve hot or at room temperature.

bacon wrapped bbq shrimp po' boy

Creamy Cole Slaw

2 cups shredded white cabbage

¾ cup shredded red cabbage

¾ cup shredded carrot

½ cup sliced sweet onion

⅓ cup honey

1 cup mayonnaise

2½ tablespoons horseradish

1 teaspoon celery salt

Freshly ground black pepper to taste

COMPLIMENTS OF:

CHEF KEVIN STOCKDALE

THE TEMPTATION

BOCA GRANDE, FLORIDA

Sandwich

12 slices applewood-smoked bacon, cut in half crosswise

24 large shrimp (16 to 20 count), peeled, deveined and tails removed

16 ounces bbq sauce

6 (6-inch) hoagie rolls

12 slices lacey Swiss cheese

For the cole slaw, combine white cabbage, red cabbage, carrots and onion; mix well. In a separate container, mix honey, mayonnaise, horseradish, celery salt and pepper. Add to slaw mixture a little at a time until you reach desired moistness and texture.

Preheat oven to 350°. For the sandwich, place the bacon on a rimmed baking sheet and bake for 8 to 10 minutes or until cooked half way.

Using ½ piece of bacon per shrimp, wrap shrimp and place on 6 bamboo skewers (4 shrimp per skewer). Baste the shrimp with bbq sauce. Grill shrimp over medium-high heat. When shrimp is cooked through, 3 to 4 minutes on each side, remove from skewer. Place on a hoagie roll and top with Swiss cheese. Bake in oven 1 to 2 minutes or until cheese melts. Top with cole slaw and remaining half of roll.

shrimp blt

1 pound large shrimp, peeled and deveined

Kosher salt and freshly ground black pepper to taste

2 ripe avocados, peeled, pitted and diced

1 small red onion, diced

¼ cup fresh lime juice

3 dashes hot pepper sauce

8 slices bread of your choice, lightly toasted

12 slices bacon, cooked until just crisp

4 romaine leaves

2 large ripe tomatoes, sliced ½-inch thick

Season the shrimp with salt and pepper and thread onto skewers. Grill over medium heat for 3 to 4 minutes per side until opaque throughout. Remove from the grill and cut each shrimp into 4 pieces; place in a bowl. Add the avocados, onion, lime juice and pepper sauce; mix together. Adjust seasoning. The mixture should form a thick and chunky paste.

Put a generous amount of this mixture on each of 4 pieces of bread, top with bacon, lettuce and tomato. Put the other pieces of bread on top and serve.

Shrimp can be sautéed in a small amount of olive oil instead of grilled.

crunchy salmon sandwich

¼ cup mayonnaise

2 tablespoons prepared horseradish

1 teaspoon chopped fresh dill

1 teaspoon chopped fresh chives

Kosher salt and freshly ground black pepper to taste

2 pieces skinless, boneless center-cut salmon fillets
   (each 3½ to 4-inches wide)

2 tablespoon olive oil

8 slices toasted caraway rye bread

4 butter lettuce leaves

4 thin slices red onion

In a small bowl, combine mayonnaise, horseradish, dill, chives, salt and pepper. Set aside.

Cut each salmon fillet in half horizontally. Heat oil in a large nonstick skillet over medium-high heat. Add salmon; sear 2 minutes or until crisp and brown. Turn salmon and cook 30 to 40 seconds or until opaque in center.

Top each of 4 slices of bread with a lettuce leaf, a piece of salmon and a red onion slice. Spread horseradish-dill mayonnaise generously on remaining slices of bread and set on top of onion.

j.t.'s fish tacos

6 (2-ounce) pieces grouper, mahi mahi or fish of choice

Cajun seasoning

½ cup peanut oil

1 cup julienned white cabbage

1 cup julienned carrots

1 cup julienned celery

1 cup julienned snow peas

1 cup julienned green onions

1 cup fresh bean sprouts

1 tablespoon red pepper flakes or to taste

¼ cup teriyaki sauce

6 taco shells (soft, deep fried or store-bought)

1 cup shredded romaine lettuce

SAUCE TOPPINGS (OPTIONAL): Sweet and sour sauce, wasabi cream, pickled ginger, Asian sweet chili sauce

COMPLIMENTS OF:

CHEF J.T. TURNER

P.J.'S SEAGRILLE

BOCA GRANDE, FLORIDA

Dust the fish with Cajun seasoning. Heat peanut oil in a large skillet and blacken fish on both sides. Fully cook fish and place on paper towels to drain.

In the same skillet, add the cabbage, carrots, celery, snow peas, green onions and bean sprouts. Quickly sauté for about 1 minute and add red pepper flakes and teriyaki sauce. Toss to combine. Remove from heat and drain vegetables in a colander.

To quickly build tacos, in each taco shell place shredded lettuce, hot sautéed vegetables (using tongs) and fish. Top with sauce of your choice.

provençale tuna sandwich

Vinaigrette

4 tablespoons extra virgin olive oil

1½ tablespoons red wine vinegar

½ teaspoon Dijon mustard

Kosher salt and freshly ground black pepper to taste

Sandwich

1 French baguette

Fresh salad greens

2 roasted red bell peppers, diced

2 roasted yellow bell peppers, diced

⅓ cup chopped black olives (preferably niçoise)

2 (5-ounce) cans best quality Italian tuna, packed in olive oil,
    drained and crumbled

2 hard-cooked eggs, sliced crosswise

6 to 8 anchovies, drained and chopped

A day in advance of serving, combine olive oil, vinegar, mustard, salt and pepper; whisk to blend.

Slice baguette in half lengthwise. On bottom half, drizzle half of the vinaigrette. Next, layer the ingredients in this order: salad greens, roasted peppers, olives, tuna, eggs and anchovies. Drizzle remaining vinaigrette over the top. Cover with the top half of the baguette. Wrap sandwich tightly with plastic. Place on a tray and top with another tray. Weigh down with something heavy, such as a gallon of milk, and refrigerate overnight.

the real deal cuban sandwich

Cuban Pork

3 heads garlic, cloves separated and peeled

2 teaspoons kosher salt

1 teaspoon black peppercorns

¾ cup fresh orange juice

⅓ cup fresh lemon juice

⅓ cup fresh lime juice

1 cup minced onion

2 teaspoons dried oregano

1 cup olive oil

1 (3 to 4 pound) boneless pork shoulder roast

Sandwich

1 French baguette

2 tablespoons butter, room temperature

4 slices Black Forest ham

4 slices Swiss cheese

4 dill pickles, sliced lengthwise

A day in advance of serving, prepare pork. Combine garlic, salt, peppercorns, juices, onion, oregano and olive oil. Place pork in a large dish and add the olive oil mixture to cover. Marinate overnight.

Drain meat, reserving marinade. Pat dry with paper towels. Brown pork in a nonstick skillet for 2 to 3 minutes on each side to seal in juices. Place browned pork and ³/₄ cup reserved marinade in a crockpot. Cook for 8 to 10 hours on low heat. Shred meat, using two forks. There will be more than needed for 4 sandwiches.

To prepare sandwiches, preheat oven to 350°. Cut bread in half lengthwise. Butter insides of both halves. Layer pork, ham, cheese and pickle slices on one side of bread. Place top of bread on sandwich and press down. To serve hot, either foil-wrap and bake for 20 to 30 minutes, grill in a buttered skillet or in a panini press. Cheese should be melted to assure that flavors are combined.

Pork and marinade can be braised in a covered Dutch oven at 325° for 3 to 4 hours until meat is tender and can be shredded.

banyan blue burger

4 ounces butter, room temperature

8 ounces blue cheese, room temperature

1/8 teaspoon cayenne pepper

2 pounds ground chuck

1 pound ground sirloin

2 tablespoons Dijon mustard

2 tablespoons steak sauce

Celery salt to taste

Freshly ground black pepper to taste

8 hamburger buns

GARNISH: Sliced tomatoes, lettuce and sliced red onion

COMPLIMENTS OF:

OWNER AND CHEF

NELSON PERKINS

COLT AND GRAY

DENVER, COLORADO

Combine well the butter and blue cheese. Stir in the cayenne pepper and form into 8 balls; flatten into "patties". Refrigerate until firm.

Meanwhile, gently mix the ground meats with the mustard and steak sauce, keeping the meat as loose as possible. When the cheese is cold, form the meat around the cheese and make uniform patties. Don't pack the burgers too tightly.

Season the burgers well with celery salt and pepper. Cook on a hot grill 4 minutes on each side (for medium-rare), turning only once. Allow the burgers to rest for 2 minutes before serving.

Gently mark the buns on the grill and serve with lettuce, tomato, red onion and condiments of your choice.

salads

hearts of palm and citrus salad

4 red grapefruit

1 tablespoon fresh lime juice

1 tablespoon sugar

¼ teaspoon ground cumin

½ cup canola oil

Kosher salt to taste

Hot pepper sauce to taste

4 avocados, peeled and cut into 1-inch pieces

1 small red onion, thinly sliced

2 (14-ounce) cans hearts of palm, drained and sliced ½-inch thick, on the diagonal

½ cup cilantro, coarsely chopped

Using a sharp knife, peel the grapefruits, removing all of the bitter white pith. Working on a cutting board, cut in between the membranes to release the sections. Cut the grapefruit sections into bite-size pieces. Squeeze the grapefruit membranes over a small bowl and reserve ¼ cup of the grapefruit juice. Whisk in the lime juice, sugar and cumin. Slowly whisk in the oil. Season the salad dressing with salt and hot pepper sauce. Taste salad dressing for desired balance between sweet and tart.

Transfer the grapefruit pieces to a large bowl. Add the avocados, onion, **hearts of palm,** cilantro and dressing. Toss gently and serve immediately.

arugula salad with apples and berries

Vinaigrette

3 tablespoons apple cider vinegar

1 teaspoon grated orange zest

2 tablespoons fresh orange juice

2½ teaspoons Dijon mustard

2 tablespoons pure maple syrup

Kosher salt and freshly ground black pepper to taste

⅔ cup extra virgin olive oil

NOTE:

CITRUS ZEST IS THE THIN, COLORED OUTER LAYER OF SKIN OF AN ORANGE, LEMON OR LIME. WHEN REMOVING THE ZEST, BE CAREFUL NOT TO INCLUDE ANY OF THE BITTER WHITE PITH.

Salad

8 ounces baby arugula

1 large Granny Smith apple, peeled and diced

½ cup toasted walnut halves, coarsely chopped

½ cup dried cranberries

6 ounces blue cheese, such as Roquefort, crumbled

8 ounces thick-cut bacon, cooked crisp and broken into
   1-inch pieces

½ teaspoon kosher salt

For the vinaigrette, whisk together the vinegar, orange zest, orange juice, mustard, maple syrup, salt and pepper in a bowl. Slowly whisk in olive oil.

To prepare the salad, in a large bowl, toss together the arugula, apple, walnuts, cranberries and blue cheese. Toss the salad with just enough vinaigrette to moisten. Add the bacon and sprinkle with salt; toss well. Serve immediately.

hearts of palm and watercress salad

Vinaigrette

2 teaspoons Dijon mustard

Juice of ½ lemon

½ cup white wine vinegar

1 cup extra virgin olive oil

½ teaspoon kosher salt

¼ teaspoon pepper

CHEF TIP:

TOP THIS **hearts of palm**
SALAD WITH GRILLED SALMON
OR CHICKEN FOR A WARM
WEATHER ENTRÉE.

Salad

½ (14-ounce) can hearts of palm

½ pound mushrooms, sliced

Juice of ½ lemon

1 bunch watercress

1 head Boston lettuce

For the vinaigrette, whisk together mustard, lemon juice, vinegar, olive oil, salt and pepper; set aside.

To prepare the salad, drain and slice **hearts of palm**. Combine with sliced mushrooms and marinate in juice of $^1/_2$ lemon.

Tear watercress leaves into small pieces and place in a salad bowl. Tear Boston lettuce into bite-sized pieces and add to watercress. Remove **hearts of palm** and mushrooms from lemon juice with slotted spoon. Add to salad greens. Toss salad mixture with desired amount of vinaigrette just before serving.

arugula, mushroom, gruyère and prosciutto salad

Lemon Mustard Cream Dressing

2 tablespoons Dijon mustard or to taste

3 to 4 tablespoons fresh lemon juice

½ cup extra virgin olive oil

¼ cup heavy cream or crème fraîche

Kosher salt and freshly ground black pepper to taste

Salad

6 large handfuls of arugula (about ½ pound)

3 heads Belgian endive, leaves separated

12 large white mushrooms, stems trimmed, sliced ⅛-inch thick

6 thin slices Gruyère or Emmenthaler cheese, cut into
    2½-inch x ⅛-inch strips

6 thin slices prosciutto, cut into 2½-inch x ⅛-inch strips

NOTE:

ARUGULA IS A PEPPERY, TENDER GREEN, ALSO KNOWN AS ROCKET, WHICH CAN BE SERVED IN A SALAD OR COOKED. USE IT IN PLACE OF BASIL FOR A SPICY PESTO SAUCE. WHEN GROWING, ITS FLAVOR CHANGES WITH THE WEATHER AND SOIL CONDITIONS. WHAT YOU BUY THIS WEEK CAN BE MILDER (OR SPICIER) THAN THE NEXT.

To make the dressing, whisk the mustard and lemon juice together in a small bowl. Gradually add the olive oil and cream or crème fraîche. Add salt and pepper to taste.

To prepare the salad, toss the greens with half the dressing and divide among 6 salad plates. Toss the mushrooms with enough dressing to coat and arrange on the greens. Lay the strips of cheese and prosciutto on top and drizzle lightly with the desired amount of dressing. Serve immediately.

avocado and watercress salad

Serves 4 to 6

3 ripe avocados, split and cut into 1-inch pieces

1 bunch watercress, stems trimmed

Juice of one lemon

¼ cup extra virgin olive oil

Kosher salt and freshly ground black pepper to taste

½ pound sliced bacon, cooked until crisp

Place avocado pieces in a salad bowl. Add watercress and drizzle with the lemon juice and olive oil. Sprinkle with salt and pepper and gently toss. Top the salad with bacon, broken into 1-inch pieces.

florida walnut salad

Serves 4

Lemon Vinaigrette

1½ teaspoons Dijon mustard

2 tablespoons fresh lemon juice

1 garlic clove, minced

⅓ cup extra virgin olive oil

Kosher salt and freshly ground black pepper to taste

Salad

2 ripe avocados, peeled and cut into 1-inch pieces

¾ cup walnuts, toasted and very coarsely chopped

1¼ cups celery, diced about ½-inch thick

1 cucumber, peeled, seeded and cut into 1-inch pieces

½ cup finely diced red onion

Mixed greens

To make the vinaigrette, combine Dijon mustard, lemon juice and garlic in a salad bowl. Whisk, slowly adding olive oil in a steady stream. Season with salt and pepper.

To prepare the salad, add the avocado, walnuts, celery, cucumber and red onion to the vinaigrette and gently toss. Put a bed of greens on each of four salad plates. Mound a serving of avocado mixture on top of greens.

bibb salad with raspberry vinaigrette

Serves 6

Vinaigrette

¼ cup raspberry vinegar

2 tablespoons maple syrup

⅔ cup canola oil

Salad

2 heads Bibb or Boston lettuce, torn in small pieces

1 small red onion, sliced and separated into rings

4 ounces crumbled blue cheese

¼ cup pine nuts, toasted

To make the vinaigrette, combine vinegar and syrup; whisk, slowly adding oil.

To prepare the salad, combine lettuce and onion; arrange on individual salad plates. Sprinkle salad with crumbled cheese and nuts. Drizzle with vinaigrette.

endive, gorgonzola and pine nut salad

Vinaigrette

½ cup canola oil

½ cup extra virgin olive oil

¼ cup balsamic vinegar

1 tablespoon chopped fresh sage

1 tablespoon chopped fresh basil

Kosher salt and freshly ground black pepper to taste

Salad

4 heads Belgium endive leaves, separated

4 ounces Gorgonzola, slightly frozen

½ cup pine nuts, toasted

For the vinaigrette, combine canola oil, olive oil, vinegar, sage, basil, salt and pepper in a jar and shake well.

To prepare the salad, place endive in a large bowl and pour vinaigrette over leaves; toss gently. Place endive in a pretty pattern on a large plate or platter and spoon additional vinaigrette over salad. Leaves should have some vinaigrette standing in them. Grate partially frozen Gorgonzola over endive. Sprinkle pine nuts over all. Salad can be passed as finger food or served on individual plates.

belgian endive and pear salad

Roquefort Cream Dressing

½ cup extra virgin olive oil

¼ cup finely crumbled Roquefort cheese

¼ cup heavy cream

2 tablespoons fresh lemon juice or to taste

Kosher salt and freshly ground black pepper to taste

Salad

1 cup walnuts, toasted and coarsely chopped

4 heads Belgian endive

2 small bulbs fennel

1 large or 2 small ripe Bartlett or Comice pears, halved, cored and thinly sliced (with peel)

To make the dressing, place olive oil, cheese, cream, lemon juice, salt and pepper in the bowl of a food processor or blender and pulse quickly just until combined. Do not over process. If the dressing is too thick, thin with water.

To prepare the salad, toss the walnuts in a small bowl with a few tablespoons of the dressing and let sit to macerate for 10 to 15 minutes.

Remove the root ends from the endive and separate the leaves; break into bite-size pieces. Cut the fennel bulbs in half, remove the tough outer leaves, cut out the cores and thinly slice the bulbs.

Combine the endive leaves and fennel in a large salad bowl. Toss with desired amount of remaining dressing. Arrange on 4 salad plates. Place the pears over the endive and fennel. Drizzle with dressing and top with the walnuts. Serve immediately.

blt salad with buttermilk-blue cheese dressing

Dressing

½ cup mayonnaise

1 tablespoon white vinegar

1 tablespoon fresh lemon juice

¼ cup whole buttermilk

2 tablespoons chopped red onion

2 tablespoons chopped fresh flat-leaf parsley

2 to 3 tablespoons crumbled blue cheese

Kosher salt and freshly ground black pepper to taste

Salad

¼ pound pancetta or bacon

2 cups mixed greens

2 cups torn romaine lettuce leaves

2 large ripe tomatoes, cored and diced

To make the dressing, whisk the mayonnaise, vinegar and lemon juice together in a small bowl. Add the buttermilk and whisk again. Stir in the onion, parsley and blue cheese. Season with salt and pepper to taste. The dressing will keep, covered, in the refrigerator for 1 day.

To prepare the salad, fry the pancetta or bacon until crisp and drain on paper towels. When cool enough to handle, crumble and set aside. Toss the greens and romaine leaves together; place in a shallow bowl or on a platter. Arrange the tomatoes over the greens, pour dressing over greens and top with the crumbled bacon. Add more fresh pepper and serve.

spinach and apple salad

Orange Dressing

½ (6-ounce) can orange juice concentrate

⅔ cup canola oil

1 tablespoon red wine vinegar

¼ cup sugar

¼ teaspoon kosher salt

¼ teaspoon dry mustard

Dash of hot pepper sauce (optional)

Salad

1 (9-ounce) package baby spinach

1 Delicious apple, sliced

2 hard-cooked eggs, chopped

1 small red onion, sliced

½ cup chopped pecans, toasted

6 slices bacon, cooked until crisp, drained and crumbled

For the Orange Dressing, mix juice concentrate, oil, vinegar, sugar, salt, mustard and pepper sauce, if using, together. Beat with electric mixer or whisk until sugar dissolves.

To prepare the salad, place spinach in a salad bowl. Add sliced apple, chopped eggs, sliced onion and pecans. Toss with orange dressing and top with crumbled bacon.

very berry spinach salad

Vinaigrette

½ **cup extra virgin olive oil**

¼ **cup red wine vinegar**

¼ **cup sugar**

2 **garlic cloves, crushed**

¼ **teaspoon kosher salt**

¼ **teaspoon freshly ground black pepper**

¼ **teaspoon dry mustard**

¼ **teaspoon onion powder**

Salad

1 **cup slivered almonds**

1 **pound baby spinach leaves, trimmed**

1 **pound baby butterhead lettuce**

1 **bunch green onions, chopped**

½ **pint fresh strawberries, sliced**

½ **pint fresh raspberries**

½ **pint fresh blueberries**

¼ **cup chopped fresh dill**

For the vinaigrette, combine the olive oil, vinegar, sugar, garlic, salt, pepper, dry mustard and onion powder in a jar with a tight-fitting lid. Shake to mix. Chill until serving time.

For the salad, preheat the oven to 350°. Spread the almonds on a baking sheet. Toast for 5 to 7 minutes or until golden brown, stirring after 3 to 4 minutes. Let stand until cool. Toss the almonds, spinach, lettuce, green onions, strawberries, raspberries, blueberries and dill in a large salad bowl. Add the vinaigrette just before serving and toss to coat.

mixed greens with fennel, pears and parmesan

Vinaigrette

½ tablespoon Dijon mustard

2 tablespoons fresh lemon juice

2 teaspoons tarragon vinegar

2 green onions, chopped

¾ cup canola oil

1 cup extra virgin olive oil

Kosher salt and freshly ground black pepper to taste

Salad

2 bunches watercress, tough stems removed

3 cups coarsely torn salad greens

1½ cups sliced fresh fennel

3 tablespoons pine nuts, toasted

2 ripe Bosc pears, peeled, cored and thinly sliced

1 cup shaved Parmesan cheese (use vegetable peeler)

To make the vinaigrette, whisk mustard with lemon juice and vinegar. Add chopped green onions. While continuing to whisk, pour in the canola oil and olive oil in a thin, steady stream. Season with salt and pepper.

To prepare the salad, toss the watercress, greens and fennel together in a large salad bowl. Scatter the pine nuts, pears and Parmesan cheese over the greens. Toss the salad with enough vinaigrette to coat. Serve immediately.

edamame salad

Vinaigrette

2 tablespoons rice vinegar

2 tablespoons fresh lemon juice

1 tablespoon canola oil

1 teaspoon minced garlic

NOTE:

EDAMAME IS THE JAPANESE NAME FOR THE VERY NUTRITIOUS WHOLE FRESH SOYBEANS WHICH ARE FOUND IN THE FREEZER OR PRODUCE SECTION OF A GROCERY STORE.

Salad

1½ cups cooked, shelled edamame beans
   (about 20-ounces of pods)

3 large carrots, coarsely grated

⅓ cup thinly sliced green onions

2 tablespoons chopped fresh cilantro

Kosher salt and freshly ground black pepper to taste

To make the vinaigrette, whisk the vinegar, lemon juice, oil and garlic in a small bowl.

To prepare the salad, toss the edamame beans, carrots, green onions and cilantro in a bowl. Add the vinaigrette to the bean mixture and toss to coat. Season with salt and pepper. Chill, covered, until serving time.

The original drugstore, now known as Fugate's Sundries, is where you can pick up your daily reserved copy of the New York Times or the Wall Street Journal, emergency Band-Aids, cough drops and an endless variety of gifts. Through the side door is a ladies dress and sportswear shop that was once occupied by the Patio Bar. For many years Mrs. Fugate went to New York on buying trips and filled her store with semi-chic and expensive clothes, sizes up to 18. Patrons still get great pleasure out of returning to Wilmington or Philadelphia or Easthampton, and upon receiving a compliment, smile and say, "Thank you, I got it at the drug store in Boca Grande."

haricot vert, goat cheese and prosciutto salad

Vinaigrette

¼ cup sherry wine vinegar

Juice of one fresh lemon

2 shallots, minced

5 tablespoons extra virgin olive oil

Salad

2 pounds fresh haricots verts (petite green beans), ends trimmed

½ pound prosciutto or pancetta, thinly sliced

4 ounces herbed goat cheese, cut into bits

Kosher salt and freshly ground black pepper to taste

To make the vinaigrette, mix vinegar, lemon juice and shallots in a bowl; whisk in olive oil.

Preheat oven to 400°. To prepare the salad, bring 3 cups water to a boil and add haricots verts. Boil for 40 seconds; drain immediately and drop into an ice bath to stop the cooking process. When haricots verts are cool, drain again and set aside.

Place prosciutto on a baking sheet in individual pieces. Bake until crisp. Let cool slightly and then chop into small pieces or strips.

Toss together green beans, goat cheese and prosciutto; add vinaigrette and toss gently. Season with salt and pepper.

corn, cherry tomato and blue cheese salad

Dressing

2 tablespoons balsamic vinegar

⅓ cup extra virgin olive oil

3 ounces blue cheese, crumbled

Salad

2¾ cups cooked fresh corn or thawed frozen corn

1 pint cherry tomatoes, cut into halves

4 celery ribs, chopped

½ large red onion, chopped

1 cup arugula, trimmed and chopped

Kosher salt and freshly ground black pepper to taste

1 ounce blue cheese, crumbled

To make the dressing, pour the balsamic vinegar into a bowl. Gradually add the olive oil, whisking constantly until blended. Stir in the blue cheese.

To prepare the salad, combine the corn, cherry tomatoes, celery and onion in a salad bowl and mix gently. The dressing and salad can be prepared 4 to 24 hours in advance and stored separately in the refrigerator.

To serve, combine arugula with corn mixture. Add the dressing, salt and pepper; toss to coat. Sprinkle with blue cheese.

marinated mushroom salad

1 to 2 lemons

4 tablespoons extra virgin olive oil, divided

2 garlic cloves, each cut in half

Kosher salt and freshly ground black pepper to taste

2 pounds small white mushrooms, trimmed and cut into quarters

½ cup loosely packed fresh parsley, chopped

3 tablespoons snipped chives

1 bag (5-ounces) baby spinach

1 bag (5-ounces) mixed baby greens

GARNISH: Chives

Pecorino Romano cheese, thinly shaved

From lemons, grate $1/2$ teaspoon zest and squeeze $1/3$ cup juice. In a 4-quart saucepan, heat lemon zest and juice, 3 tablespoons oil, garlic, salt and pepper to boiling on high. Reduce heat to medium and simmer 30 seconds. Stir in mushrooms, parsley and chives. Transfer to a large zip-top plastic bag. Seal bag, pressing out excess air. Place bag in bowl and refrigerate 6 hours or overnight.

Place sieve over a salad bowl; drain mushrooms over bowl (reserving marinade). Discard garlic cloves; set mushrooms aside. Add remaining 1 tablespoon oil to marinade in bowl; whisk until blended. Add spinach and mixed greens; toss to combine. Place greens on individual salad plates and top with mushrooms.

Garnish with snipped chives and Pecorino Romano shavings.

bean and feta salad

Vinaigrette

2 cloves garlic, minced

1½ tablespoons coarse-grained Dijon mustard

⅓ cup fresh lemon juice

1¼ cups extra virgin olive oil

1½ teaspoons kosher salt

½ teaspoon freshly ground black pepper

VARIATION:

CANNED BLACK BEANS
AND/OR GARBANZO BEANS
CAN BE SUBSTITUTED FOR THE
NAVY BEANS.

Beans

1 pound dried white navy beans, soaked in cold water overnight,
   drained

6 cups water

3 carrots, chopped

2 bay leaves

Salad

¾ cup finely chopped red onion

4 ounces feta cheese, crumbled

½ cup pine nuts, lightly toasted

1 cup chopped parsley

To make the vinaigrette, in a small bowl mix together garlic, mustard and lemon juice. Pouring in a steady stream, whisk in olive oil. Add salt and pepper.

Combine beans, water, carrots and bay leaves in a large saucepan. Heat to boiling, skimming foam from surface. Reduce heat and simmer, uncovered, until beans are tender but not mushy, 25 to 30 minutes. Remove from heat and drain, discarding carrots and bay leaves.

To prepare the salad, toss beans with the desired amount of vinaigrette. Add onion, cheese, pine nuts and parsley. Toss to combine well. Serve at room temperature.

petite pea salad

Dressing

¼ teaspoon dry mustard

2 tablespoons sour cream

¾ teaspoon kosher salt

⅛ teaspoon freshly ground black pepper

1 garlic clove, minced

2½ tablespoons red wine vinegar

½ cup canola oil

Salad

10 ounces frozen petite peas, thawed

1 cup diced celery

4 slices bacon, cooked until crisp and crumbled

¼ cup sliced green onion

1 cup macadamia nuts, coarsely chopped

To make the dressing, whisk the dry mustard, sour cream, salt, pepper, garlic and vinegar. Gradually whisk in the canola oil until well combined. Chill dressing for at least 4 hours.

To prepare the salad, toss the peas, celery, bacon, onion and nuts with the desired amount of dressing; chill.

island panzanella salad

Vinaigrette

2 garlic cloves, minced

1 teaspoon dried oregano

½ teaspoon Dijon mustard

¼ cup red wine vinegar

½ cup extra virgin olive oil

1 teaspoon kosher salt

½ teaspoon freshly ground black pepper

Salad

3 tablespoons extra virgin olive oil

6 cups (1-inch cubes) French or Italian bread

Kosher salt and freshly ground black pepper to taste

1 cucumber, unpeeled

1 red bell pepper, diced in ½-inch pieces

1 yellow bell pepper, diced in ½-inch pieces

1 pint cherry or grape tomatoes, halved

½ small red onion, thinly sliced

½ pound feta cheese, cubed

½ cup kalamata olives, pitted and halved

To prepare vinaigrette, place the garlic, oregano, mustard and vinegar in a small bowl and whisk together. Whisking constantly, slowly add the olive oil to make an emulsion. Add salt and pepper.

To prepare the salad, heat 3 tablespoons of olive oil in a large sauté pan. Add the bread and sprinkle with salt; cook over low to medium heat, tossing frequently, for 5 to 10 minutes, until nicely browned. Set aside.

Cut the cucumber in half lengthwise and scoop out the seeds with a small spoon. Discard the seeds and slice the cucumber ¼-inch thick; place in a large bowl. Add the red bell pepper, yellow bell pepper, tomatoes, red onion, feta, olives and bread cubes to the bowl. Add the vinaigrette and toss lightly. Set aside for 30 minutes for the flavors to blend. Serve at room temperature.

shrimp and fennel salad

2½ tablespoons olive oil, divided

1 large red bell pepper, diced

1 medium fennel bulb, trimmed and diced

¼ teaspoon red pepper flakes, divided

Kosher salt to taste

Juice of 1 lemon, divided

1 pound large shrimp, peeled and deveined

1 garlic clove, minced

3 green onions, sliced

1 tablespoon drained capers

1 teaspoon mayonnaise

2 to 3 teaspoons minced fresh rosemary

Heat 1 tablespoon of oil in a large skillet over high heat. Add bell pepper, fennel, half of the crushed pepper flakes and salt to taste. Cook, stirring often, until vegetables begin to brown at the edges, 6 to 7 minutes. Transfer to a mixing bowl and add half of the lemon juice.

Add 1 tablespoon oil to pan. When hot, add shrimp, remaining pepper flakes and salt to taste. Cook, stirring, until shrimp are pink, 2 to 3 minutes, adding remaining lemon juice and garlic. Add to vegetables. Add onions, capers, mayonnaise, rosemary and the remaining ½ tablespoon oil; mix well.

The salad can be served when it cools to room temperature or chilled overnight. Adjust the seasoning at serving time.

thai shrimp salad with honey-lime vinaigrette

Honey-Lime Vinaigrette

⅓ cup fresh lime juice

¼ cup honey

¼ cup brown sugar

½ bunch fresh cilantro, chopped

¾ cup canola oil

2 teaspoons kosher salt

½ teaspoon freshly ground black pepper

2 tablespoons freshly grated ginger

COMPLIMENTS OF:

CHEF TOM O'SHIELDS

3RD STREET CAFÉ

BOCA GRANDE, FLORIDA

Shrimp Salad

12 large shrimp (16 to 20 count), peeled and deveined with the tails on

¼ cup unsweetened coconut milk

2 tablespoons fresh lime juice

1 tablespoon sugar

1½ teaspoons chopped garlic

1 tablespoon soy sauce

1 tablespoon chopped fresh cilantro

1 tablespoon canola or peanut oil

1½ teaspoons chopped fresh ginger

Mixed greens

Sweet Asian chili sauce

For the dressing, mix together lime juice, honey, brown sugar and cilantro in the bowl of a food processor. Blend well and then slowly add oil in a steady stream. Add salt, pepper and ginger. Pulse to combine.

For the shrimp, skewer each shrimp through the tail and up to the head but do not let skewer come out of the head. Skewered shrimp should look like a lollipop.

Mix together coconut milk, lime juice, sugar, garlic, soy sauce, cilantro, oil and ginger.

Pour over shrimp and marinate for at least 1 hour and preferably 6 hours.

Grill shrimp over hot coals 2 to 3 minutes on each side. Do not overcook, as they will become extremely tough.

Mix favorite greens with vinaigrette and mound them in the center of each of 4 plates.

Stand 3 skewered, grilled shrimp around each mound of greens, creating a "tepee" effect. Drizzle a small amount of sweet chili sauce between each skewer.

Wrapping the southeast corner of downtown Boca Grande is Whidden's Marina, an island treasure that has recently been added to the National Historic Register. Visitors are charmed by the collection of old cars and rusty bikes parked randomly around the long box of pink plastic flowers, two Vietnamese pigs that grunt longingly at passersby for food, stray cats snoozing in the sun, and all manner of debris that defies description. Inside the weathered gray building, its floor wavy with age and water damage, Isabel Joiner still reigns. She answers the phone daily, relaying information concerning the arrival of the "shrimp boat". Normally a weekend event, the shrimp boat ties up at the back of the dock and sells upward of two hundred pounds of fresh shrimp in a half day. At $8 per pound for "boat run" shrimp and $10 for jumbo shrimp, it is the freshest, most delicious shrimp in the world—sold by a colorful, beer-sipping crew.

summertime shrimp salad

Dressing

1 cup mayonnaise

1 tablespoon orange zest (2 oranges)

2 tablespoons fresh orange juice

1 tablespoon white wine vinegar

½ teaspoon kosher salt

½ teaspoon freshly ground black pepper

Salad

2 quarts water

½ teaspoon kosher salt

2½ pounds medium shrimp

¼ cup minced fresh dill

¼ cup capers, drained

2 tablespoons small-diced red onion

To make the dressing, in a large bowl, whisk together the mayonnaise, orange zest, orange juice, vinegar, salt and pepper.

To prepare the salad, bring water and salt to a boil; add shrimp and cook approximately 3 minutes. Drain and run under cold water. Peel, devein and coarsely chop shrimp. Add shrimp to dressing and toss. Add dill, capers and red onion; toss to combine and chill.

gulf shrimp and cannellini bean salad

Shrimp

4 cups water

⅓ cup parsley sprigs

2 garlic cloves, peeled

1 onion, quartered

1 bay leaf

1½ pounds medium shrimp, peeled and deveined

NOTE:
2 POUNDS HEADS-ON SHRIMP
EQUAL 1 POUND SHRIMP.

Salad

2 tablespoons extra virgin olive oil

¼ teaspoon kosher salt

¼ teaspoon freshly ground black pepper

2 garlic cloves, minced

¾ cup diced red bell pepper

½ cup diced avocado

½ cup minced fresh cilantro

¼ cup fresh lime juice

2 (15-ounce) cans cannellini beans or other white beans, rinsed and drained

To prepare shrimp, combine the water, parsley, garlic, onion and bay leaf in a medium saucepan. Bring to a boil; add shrimp, and cook 3 minutes or until shrimp are done. Drain and rinse with cold water; cool. Discard onion, garlic and herbs.

To prepare the salad, combine oil, salt, pepper and garlic; stir well with a whisk. Add shrimp, bell pepper, avocado, cilantro, lime juice and beans; toss well. Cover and chill 1 hour.

Lovely for a luncheon or as part of a buffet.

scallop salad with warm catalan vinaigrette

Catalan Vinaigrette

2 tablespoons sherry vinegar

2 tablespoons fresh orange juice

⅓ cup sliced almonds, toasted and coarsely chopped

1 tablespoon capers, rinsed and chopped

1 tablespoon grated orange zest

1½ teaspoons puréed or finely chopped anchovies

Kosher salt and freshly ground black pepper to taste

½ cup extra virgin olive oil

NOTE:

½ TEASPOON ANCHOVY
PASTE (AVAILABLE IN A TUBE)
IS THE EQUIVALENT OF 1
ANCHOVY FILLET.

Salad

1½ cups thinly sliced white or cremini mushrooms

4 handfuls of mixed salad greens (about ⅓ pound)

Kosher salt to taste

16 large or 24 small sea scallops

To make the vinaigrette, whisk together vinegar, orange juice, almonds, capers, orange zest, anchovies, salt and pepper in a bowl. Gradually whisk in olive oil. As this vinaigrette is a bit chunky, thin it with more oil if necessary to achieve the desired consistency.

To prepare the salad, toss the mushrooms in a bowl with about ¼ cup of the vinaigrette. Place the greens in a large salad bowl and salt lightly.

Sprinkle the scallops with salt. Warm ½ cup vinaigrette in a large sauté pan and cook the scallops quickly, until opaque but still quite soft and tender, about 3 minutes. Add the mushrooms to the greens and toss well. Arrange on 4 salad plates. Top with the scallops and their vinaigrette and serve while the scallops are still warm.

tuna and white bean salad

Pesto Sauce

1 small garlic clove

½ cup packed flat-leaf parsley

¼ cup packed fresh basil

1½ tablespoons fresh oregano

¼ cup capers, drained

2 tablespoons pine nuts

¼ cup extra virgin olive oil

1 teaspoon fresh lemon juice

Kosher salt and freshly ground black pepper to taste

Salad

3 (5-ounce) cans best quality Italian tuna packed in olive oil, drained

2 (15-ounce) cans cannellini beans, drained and rinsed

3 heads Belgian endive, thinly sliced crosswise

To prepare pesto, in the bowl of a food processor, combine the garlic, parsley, basil and oregano; pulse until the herbs are coarsely chopped. Add the capers and pine nuts; pulse until they are coarsely chopped. Add the olive oil and lemon juice; pulse until the pesto comes together but is still chunky. Season with salt and pepper.

To prepare the salad, in a large bowl, break up the tuna into bite-size chunks. Add the cannellini beans, sliced endives and pesto. Toss gently until the salad is evenly coated. Season with salt and pepper. The tossed salad can be refrigerated for up to 4 hours.

palm island crabmeat salad

1 pound fresh lump crabmeat

¾ cup chopped celery

2 tablespoons lemon juice

1 teaspoon grated lemon zest

1 teaspoon kosher salt

Freshly ground black pepper to taste

3 tablespoons mayonnaise

1 teaspoon capers

Salad greens

GARNISH: Grape tomatoes

Combine crabmeat, celery, lemon juice, lemon zest, salt, pepper, mayonnaise and capers. Mix gently and refrigerate. Serve on a bed of salad greens. Garnish with grape tomatoes.

cranberry relish

3 cups water

6 cups sugar

12 whole cloves

12 whole allspice

8 cinnamon sticks

4 bags whole fresh cranberries, washed

Zest of 2 oranges or Meyer lemons

Bring water, sugar, cloves, allspice and cinnamon sticks to a boil. Add fresh cranberries. Cook, stirring, until cranberries pop open; remove from heat and cool. Add zest and stir.

When cool, put in jars.

NOTE:

FOR A HUGELY SUCCESSFUL CHRISTMAS OR THANKSGIVING HOSTESS GIFT, PUT RELISH IN DECORATIVE JARS AND ATTACH A CINNAMON STICK TO THE TOP OF THE JAR WITH A PRETTY RIBBON.

beef tenderloin paillards with green salad

2 (6-ounce) beef tenderloin fillets, slightly frozen

1 to 2 garlic cloves, peeled

¼ teaspoon kosher salt

1 tablespoon fresh lemon juice

2 tablespoons extra virgin olive oil

Kosher salt and freshly ground black pepper to taste

1½ tablespoons canola oil, divided

1 bunch watercress or mixed greens

NOTE:

A PAILLARD IS A SCALLOP OF BEEF (ALSO PORK, VEAL OR CHICKEN) THAT IS QUICKLY GRILLED OR SAUTÉED.

Cut each steak horizontally into 3 equal slices. Gently pound steaks between sheets of plastic wrap to ¼-inch thickness. Mash garlic and salt together using mortar and pestle (or the side of knife blade). Whisk in lemon juice and then olive oil. Set aside.

Pat 2 paillards dry with paper towels and season with salt and pepper. Heat ¾ tablespoon of canola oil in a 10-inch heavy skillet over high heat until very hot. Sauté paillards, turning once, 1 minute a side for medium rare. Remove to a platter. Dry, season and sauté remaining paillards in the same manner with the remaining oil. Serve paillards topped with greens that have been tossed with the lemon and olive oil mixture.

apricot chicken salad with mustard mayonnaise

Mustard Mayonnaise

2 egg yolks

2 tablespoons fresh lemon juice

2 tablespoons Dijon mustard

¾ cup canola oil

⅔ cup extra virgin olive oil

¼ cup honey mustard

Kosher salt and freshly ground black pepper to taste

Salad

**3 pounds boneless, skinless chicken breasts, poached until tender
    and cooled or one whole rotisserie chicken, skinned and boned**

1 cup dried apricots, cut into ¼-inch strips

⅓ cup sherry

3 celery ribs, coarsely chopped

4 green onions, sliced diagonally

½ cup slivered almonds, toasted

1 to 3 teaspoons chopped fresh rosemary

GARNISH: Fresh rosemary sprigs

To make mayonnaise, place egg yolks, lemon juice and Dijon
mustard in the bowl of a food processor fitted with a steel blade.
Process for 10 seconds. With machine running, slowly add canola
and olive oils in a thin, steady stream through the feed tube. Add
honey mustard and process until smooth. Season with salt and pepper.

To prepare the salad, slice poached chicken breasts in 2 x ³/₄-inch
strips and place in a large mixing bowl. In a small saucepan, bring
the apricots and sherry to a boil. Reduce heat and simmer 3 minutes.
Add mixture to the chicken. Add celery, green onions, almonds and
rosemary. Toss and combine salad with dressing; chill for at least
2 hours before serving. Transfer to a serving bowl and garnish with
rosemary sprigs.

The salad can be made a day in advance but do not toss salad with
mayonnaise until a few hours before serving.

greek bulgur salad with chicken

4½ cups water

3 cups uncooked medium bulgur, rinsed

¾ cup fresh lemon juice, divided

2 teaspoons kosher salt, divided

2½ cups cubed rotisserie chicken

2½ cups peeled, chopped cucumber

2 cups halved grape tomatoes

1 cup chopped parsley

½ cup sliced basil

½ cup chopped red onion

½ cup (2-ounces) feta cheese, crumbled

¼ cup extra virgin olive oil

½ teaspoon freshly ground black pepper

10 kalamata olives, pitted and chopped

Combine water, bulgur, ½ cup lemon juice and 1 teaspoon salt in a large saucepan. Bring to a boil over medium heat; cover, reduce heat and simmer 5 minutes. Remove from heat and let stand 15 minutes. Uncover and cool to room temperature.

Combine remaining lemon juice and salt. Toss with bulgur. Add chicken, cucumber, tomatoes, parsley, basil, onion, feta, olive oil, pepper and olives. Chill.

pacific rim chicken salad with crunchy vegetables

Low-Fat Sweet and Sour Sesame Dressing

½ cup sugar

¾ teaspoon kosher salt

½ teaspoon freshly ground black pepper

½ cup white wine vinegar

1 tablespoon canola oil

1½ teaspoons Asian sesame oil

1½ tablespoons sesame seeds, toasted

Salad

4 cups thinly sliced romaine lettuce

3 cups thinly sliced Napa cabbage

½ cup very thinly sliced red cabbage

½ cup finely julienned carrots

½ cup very thinly sliced celery

1 cup peeled and seeded cucumber half-moons

1 (6-ounce) can sliced water chestnuts, drained well

3 cups thinly sliced cooked chicken breast

GARNISH: Chopped peanuts

Green onions, cut into thin diagonal slices

Mixed black and white sesame seeds, toasted

CHEF TIP:

FOR PERFECTLY POACHED CHICKEN BREASTS, FILL A SAUCEPAN WITH WATER AND ADD A FEW SPLASHES OF WHITE WINE OR LEMON JUICE. ADD SEVERAL ONION OR LEMON SLICES, CELERY LEAVES AND PARSLEY SPRIGS. SEASON WITH A DASH OF SALT AND A GRINDING OF BLACK PEPPER. ADD CHICKEN BREASTS AND BRING THE WATER TO A FULL BOIL; TURN THE HEAT OFF, LETTING THE HEAT OF THE LIQUID FINISH THE COOKING PROCESS. COOL COMPLETELY BEFORE REMOVING THE CHICKEN.

THIS METHOD KEEPS THE BREAST MEAT ESPECIALLY MOIST AND TENDER. SAVE THE STRAINED POACHING LIQUID FOR STOCK.

For the dressing, in a small bowl whisk together the sugar, salt, pepper, vinegar, canola oil, sesame oil and sesame seeds. Dressing keeps for a couple of weeks in the refrigerator.

In a large bowl, toss the romaine, cabbages, carrot, celery, cucumber, water chestnuts and chicken. Drizzle with the dressing and toss again. Divide among serving plates and garnish with peanuts, green onions and sesame seeds.

composed duck salad with raspberry vinaigrette

Marinade and Duck

1 cup dry red wine

2 tablespoons honey

2 garlic cloves, minced

¼ cup olive oil

3 thyme sprigs

6 duck breast halves

Salad

Mixed butter lettuce greens

Julienned pea pods

Orange segments

Fresh raspberries

Spicy Bourbon Pecans (see page 20) or toasted pecans

Raspberry Vinaigrette (see page 91)

To make the marinade, whisk together wine, honey, garlic and olive oil; add thyme. Place duck breasts in a glass baking dish and pour marinade over duck. Cover and marinate overnight in the refrigerator.

Remove the duck from the marinade, pat dry with paper towels and score the skin on a grill or in a grill pan. Cook the duck, skin side down, for 3 to 5 minutes. Turn and grill until the internal temperature is 125°. Let the duck cool 10 minutes; slice on the diagonal.

For the salad, arrange greens, pea pods, orange segments, raspberries and pecans on six plates. Arrange duck slices on top. Drizzle with desired amount of Raspberry Vinaigrette.

meat

terrorized steak and cherry tomato confit

Cherry Tomato Confit

1½ pounds cherry or grape tomatoes

1 cup olive oil

3 (3-inch) sprigs fresh rosemary

6 fresh thyme sprigs

6 garlic cloves, peeled

Kosher salt and freshly ground black pepper to taste

2 teaspoons red wine vinegar

1 teaspoon chopped fresh thyme

"Terror" Seasoning

¼ cup minced fresh oregano

¼ cup minced fresh rosemary

8 garlic cloves, minced

1 teaspoon kosher salt

1 teaspoon red pepper flakes

2 tablespoons cognac

2 tablespoons olive oil

1 tablespoon freshly ground black pepper

CHEF TIP:

YOU CAN SAVE THE OIL DRAINED FROM THE TOMATOES AND USE IT TO MAKE VINAIGRETTE OR DRIZZLE IT OVER ROASTED OR GRILLED VEGETABLES AND FISH. THIS CONFIT CAN BE PREPARED UP TO 5 DAYS IN ADVANCE.

Steak

4 bone-in New York strip steaks, each about 1½-inches thick

1 lemon, cut into wedges

Preheat oven to 225°. For the confit, arrange tomatoes in a baking pan large enough to hold them in a single layer. Pour the olive oil over the tomatoes, and add the rosemary, thyme sprigs and garlic. Season generously with salt and pepper. Roast slowly, uncovered, until the tomatoes are swollen and the skins are wrinkled, about 3 hours.

Remove the tomatoes from the oven and let cool. For best flavor, refrigerate tomatoes overnight and then bring back to room temperature when ready to serve.

To serve, pour tomatoes into a strainer set over a bowl, reserving both tomatoes and the oil. Discard herb sprigs and garlic. Put tomatoes in a bowl. Add the vinegar, chopped thyme and one tablespoon of the reserved oil. Mix gently taking care not to break up the tomatoes.

To make the "terror" seasoning, combine oregano, rosemary, garlic, salt, red pepper flakes, cognac, olive oil and black pepper to form a coarse paste. Rub the paste evenly on both sides of the steaks. Let the steaks marinate at room temperature for 30 to 45 minutes, or in the refrigerator for one to two hours.

Prepare a medium-hot fire on a grill. Grill the steaks until crusty on both sides, about 5 minutes on the first side and 4 minutes on the second side for medium-rare. Let steaks rest briefly. Serve with wedge of lemon and Tomato Cherry Confit.

As an alternative, steaks can be prepared in a grill pan or broiler.

savory pot roast

Serves 8 to 10

3 to 5 pound chuck or rump roast

Flour

Kosher salt and freshly ground black pepper to taste

2 tablespoons olive oil

1 tablespoon dried thyme

1 tablespoon dried basil

1 tablespoon celery salt

4 garlic cloves, chopped

1 heaping tablespoon refrigerated beef concentrate dissolved in
   1 cup water

2 cups hearty red wine

CHEF TIP:

FOR A COMPLETE MEAL-IN-A-POT, ADD CARROTS, ONIONS AND POTATOES FOR THE LAST 45 MINUTES OF COOKING. THE ROAST IS ALSO DELICIOUS SERVED OVER COOKED NOODLES AND SMOTHERED WITH THE GRAVY.

Preheat over to 350°. Lightly flour and liberally salt and pepper roast. Brown in olive oil. Add thyme, basil, celery salt and garlic. Pour beef stock and wine over meat. Liquid should be half way up side of meat, but not covering it. Add more beef concentrate and water if necessary. Braise in tightly covered casserole dish for 3 hours.

seared flank steak and salsa verde

Salsa Verde

⅔ cup flat-leaf parsley

1 garlic clove, minced

6 anchovy fillets

2 tablespoons drained capers

1 teaspoon red wine vinegar

½ cup extra virgin olive oil

Flank Steak

1½ pounds flank steak, lightly scored on both sides

1 tablespoon extra virgin olive oil

Kosher salt and freshly ground black pepper to taste

To make salsa verde, in the bowl of a food processor or blender, pulse the parsley, garlic, anchovies, capers and vinegar until coarsely chopped. With the processor running, slowly pour in the oil and mix just until blended.

For the flank steak, in a large nonstick skillet, heat 1 tablespoon of oil until almost smoking. Season the steak with salt and pepper; add it to the skillet. Cook the steak over moderately high heat until well seared outside and still pink inside, 4 to 5 minutes per side for medium-rare. Transfer to a cutting board and let stand for 5 minutes. Carve the steak across the grain into thin slices. Serve with the Salsa Verde.

This steak can be grilled.

blackened beef tenderloin
with brussels sprouts and port wine reduction

2 cups port wine

4 (5 to 7-ounce) beef tenderloin steaks

4 tablespoons Cajun seasoning

5 tablespoons extra virgin olive oil, divided

4 cups Brussels sprouts, cored and sliced

Kosher salt and freshly ground black pepper to taste

4 tablespoons blue cheese, softened and crumbled

COMPLIMENTS OF:

CHEF ETHAN SNIDER

BOCA GRANDE CLUB

BOCA GRANDE, FLORIDA

Place port wine in a small pan on medium-high heat and simmer until very thick and syrup-like; reserve.

Dredge beef with Cajun seasoning. Heat one sauté pan on high heat with 1 tablespoon extra virgin olive oil. Place beef in hot pan searing on all sides. You are looking for a very dark, almost black color on the beef. When beef is totally seared, turn down heat and continue to cook, turning often, for 6 to 8 minutes.

In a second sauté pan, set over medium-high heat, add 4 tablespoons olive oil. Add Brussels sprouts and season with salt and pepper; cook sprouts quickly, not letting them wilt. Beef should be medium rare at this point. Take beef out of pan and let rest for 5 minutes.

Place warm Brussels sprouts on each serving plate and sprinkle with crumbled blue cheese. Slice each piece of beef in three slices and place next to Brussels sprouts; drizzle port wine reduction on and around beef.

short ribs provençale

Short Ribs

2 tablespoons (or more) olive oil

6 pounds meaty beef short ribs

Kosher salt and freshly ground black pepper to taste

1 large onion, finely chopped

1 medium carrot, finely chopped

1 celery rib, finely chopped

12 whole garlic cloves, peeled

2 tablespoons flour

1 tablespoon dried herbes de Provence

2 cups red Zinfandel

2½ cups canned beef stock, divided

1 (14.5-ounce) can diced tomatoes, undrained

1 bay leaf

24 baby carrots, peeled

½ cup niçoise olives, pitted

3 tablespoons chopped fresh parsley

Preheat oven to 325°. Heat 2 tablespoons oil in heavy large ovenproof pan over medium-high heat. Sprinkle ribs with salt and pepper. Working in batches, add ribs to pan and brown well, turning often, about 8 minutes per batch. Using tongs, transfer ribs to a large bowl.

Pour off all but 2 tablespoons drippings from pan or add oil as necessary to measure 2 tablespoons. Add onion, carrot and celery and cook over medium-low heat until vegetables are soft, stirring frequently, about 10 minutes. Add garlic, flour and herbes de Provence; stir 1 minute. Add wine and 2 cups stock; bring to boil over high heat, scraping up browned bits. Add tomatoes with juices and bay leaf. Return ribs and any accumulated juices to pan. If necessary, add enough water to barely cover ribs. Bring to boil. Cover pan tightly and transfer to oven. Bake until ribs are very tender, stirring occasionally, about 2 hours 15 minutes.

Increase oven temperature to 350°. Add remaining ¹/₂ cup stock, peeled baby carrots and niçoise olives to pan; press carrots gently to submerge. Cover, return to oven and continue cooking until carrots are tender, about 15 minutes. Discard bay leaf. Transfer short ribs and carrots to a platter. Tent with foil to keep warm. If necessary, boil sauce to thicken slightly. Season to taste with salt and pepper. Pour sauce over short ribs and sprinkle with parsley.

herbes de provence

3 tablespoons dried marjoram

3 tablespoons dried thyme

1 tablespoon dried savory

1 tablespoon dried basil

1 teaspoon dried rosemary

½ teaspoon dried sage

½ teaspoon fennel seeds

Combine the herbs, mix well and spoon into a jar. Share with your "gourmet" friends.

beef bourguignon

¾ cup flour

2 teaspoons kosher salt

1 teaspoon freshly ground black pepper

5 pounds beef chuck, cut into 1½-inch pieces

¼ cup butter

¼ cup olive oil

⅓ cup cognac

½ pound bacon, diced

3 garlic cloves, mashed

4 carrots, coarsely chopped

2 leeks, coarsely chopped

2 large onions, chopped

2 tablespoons chopped fresh parsley

1 teaspoon thyme

1 bay leaf

3½ cups Burgundy wine

3 cups beef stock, divided

30 small white onions

4 tablespoons butter, divided

1 tablespoon sugar

1½ pounds mushrooms

Juice of ½ lemon

Kosher salt and freshly ground black pepper to taste

GARNISH: Chopped parsley

NOTE:

THIS IS A FAVORITE RECIPE
FROM BOCA GRANDE
ENTERTAINS.

Combine flour, salt and pepper. Dredge meat in flour mixture. In a large skillet, brown meat on all sides in butter and olive oil. Place meat in a 5-quart casserole. Deglaze skillet by pouring warmed cognac into it, stirring to loosen particles. Flame cognac and pour over meat.

Preheat oven to 350°. In the same skillet, add bacon, garlic, carrots, leeks, onions and parsley. Cook stirring, until bacon and vegetables are lightly browned. Add thyme and bay leaf to skillet, stir and add to beef. Add wine and enough beef stock to barely cover meat. Cover and bake 2 hours. Stir occasionally and add more beef stock if necessary.

To peel the white onions, drop them in boiling water for 1 minute. Cut off the ends and slip off the outer skin. Sauté the onions in 2 tablespoons butter with sugar, shaking the pan to caramelize the onions. Add a small amount of stock or water and simmer for 5 minutes. Sauté the mushrooms in remaining 2 tablespoons butter until lightly browned; sprinkle with lemon juice. Add mushrooms and onions to beef and cook 1 more hour or until beef is tender. Skim any fat from surface and remove bay leaf. Taste for salt and pepper. Serve sprinkled with chopped parsley.

grandchildren's casserole

Serves 6 to 8

1 (8-ounce) package reduced-fat cream cheese, room temperature

2 cups reduced-fat sour cream

3 green onions, chopped

1½ pounds ground chuck

2 tablespoons butter or olive oil

2 (8-ounce) cans tomato sauce

1 teaspoon Worcestershire sauce

1 teaspoon sugar

1 teaspoon kosher salt

Freshly ground black pepper to taste

1 (12-ounce) package egg noodles

2 cups grated sharp Cheddar cheese

Preheat oven to 350°. Mix cream cheese, sour cream and green onions. Set aside.

Brown meat in butter or olive oil. Add tomato sauce, Worcestershire sauce, sugar, salt and pepper.

Cook noodles al dente. In a 2-quart casserole, alternate layers of noodles, beef mixture and cream cheese mixture. Top with Cheddar cheese. Bake for 30 to 40 minutes until brown.

kid-friendly

four star chili

2 tablespoons olive oil

2 cups chopped onion

1 cup chopped green bell pepper

8 garlic cloves, minced

2 jalapeño peppers, seeded and chopped

1 pound hot Italian sausage (casings removed)

2 pounds ground sirloin

4 tablespoons chili powder

4 tablespoons brown sugar

2 tablespoons ground cumin

6 tablespoons tomato paste

2 teaspoons dried oregano

1 teaspoon freshly ground black pepper

½ teaspoon kosher salt

4 bay leaves

2 cups fruity red wine

2 (28-ounce) cans diced tomatoes, undrained

3 (16-ounce) cans kidney beans or great Northern beans, drained

1 cup shredded sharp Cheddar cheese

VARIATION:

FOR A TASTY CHANGE, USE
1 POUND GROUND BEEF
CHUCK AND 1 POUND
BONELESS SIRLOIN STEAK CUT
INTO ¼-INCH DICE INSTEAD
OF THE GROUND SIRLOIN.

Heat a large pot over medium-high heat; add the olive oil, onions, green bell pepper, garlic and jalapeño peppers. Sauté until vegetables are tender. Add sausage and ground sirloin; cook until the sausage and beef are brown, stirring to crumble. Pour off any excess fat. Add chili powder, brown sugar, ground cumin, tomato paste, oregano, pepper, salt and bay leaves. Cook for about a minute, stirring constantly. Add wine, tomatoes and kidney beans; bring to a boil. Cover and simmer 1 hour, stirring occasionally. Uncover and cook for 30 minutes, stirring occasionally. Remove the bay leaves. Serve with shredded cheese.

butterflied pork tenderloin
with honey, mustard and rosemary

2 tablespoons honey

2 tablespoons Dijon mustard

2 (4-inch) sprigs of fresh rosemary, stems removed and needles
**   crushed lightly to release flavor**

1 teaspoon kosher salt

1 tablespoon black peppercorns, crushed

1 tablespoon black mustard seeds
**   (optional, available at Asian markets)**

2 tablespoons olive oil

1 (1 pound) pork tenderloin, trimmed and butterflied

Combine the honey, mustard, rosemary, salt, pepper, mustard seeds and olive oil in a shallow dish large enough to hold the pork tenderloin. Add the tenderloin, turn to coat and marinate for at least one hour. Prepare the grill or broiler on high. Cook the pork until golden brown on all sides and firm to the touch, about 8 to 12 minutes total cooking time. Let the tenderloin rest on a cutting board for a few minutes; cut it on the diagonal into thin slices and serve.

CHEF TIP:

TO BUTTERFLY A TENDERLOIN, CUT THREE-QUARTERS OF THE WAY THROUGH THE TENDERLOIN AND OPEN UP LIKE A BOOK. BUTTERFLYING THE TENDERLOIN GIVES A LARGER SURFACE FOR THE MARINADE TO PENETRATE AND ALLOWS YOU TO GRILL OR BROIL THE MEAT QUICKLY, KEEPING IT MOIST AND TENDER.

soy-marinated pork tenderloin with shiitake cream

2 tablespoons chopped fresh ginger

2 tablespoons chopped cilantro

2 tablespoons chopped basil

¼ cup sake

¼ cup soy sauce

2 (1 pound) pork tenderloins

1 tablespoon canola oil

½ cup sliced shiitake mushrooms

2 tablespoons chopped green onions

½ cup heavy cream

⅓ cup chicken stock

Kosher salt and freshly ground black pepper

CHEF TIP:

GINGERED SWEET POTATOES
(SEE RECIPE PAGE 233)
COMPLEMENT THE FLAVORS OF
THIS DISH.

To prepare marinade, combine ginger, cilantro, basil, sake and soy sauce in a blender. Purée until smooth. Place pork in a large bowl and pour soy mixture over. Cover and refrigerate 4 to 6 hours.

Preheat oven to 350°. Coat bottom of a roasting pan with oil or nonstick spray. Transfer pork from marinade to pan, reserving ¼ cup marinade. Roast pork until internal temperature reaches 140°, about 25 minutes; do not overcook. Center should remain slightly pink.

While pork is roasting, prepare shiitake cream. In a skillet over medium heat, heat 1 tablespoon oil and add mushrooms and green onions. Sauté until mushrooms are softened, about 2 minutes. Add reserved marinade, heavy cream and chicken stock. Simmer until liquid has been reduced to ¾ of its original volume. Season with salt and pepper to taste, and keep warm.

To serve, thinly slice pork and place on 4 plates. Drizzle shiitake cream sauce over pork.

pork tenderloin with pineapple salsa

Pineapple Salsa

3 cups diced fresh pineapple

1 small red onion, finely chopped

1 jalapeño pepper, seeded and minced

2 tablespoons julienned fresh mint or cilantro

2 tablespoons fresh lime juice

Kosher salt and freshly ground black pepper to taste

Pork

2 (1 pound) pork tenderloins, trimmed

⅓ cup soy sauce

⅓ cup Dijon mustard

⅓ cup honey

1 garlic clove, minced

To make pineapple salsa, combine pineapple, red onion, jalapeño, mint or cilantro, lime juice, salt and pepper in a small bowl and set aside for 30 minutes.

To prepare the pork, combine soy sauce, mustard, honey and garlic; pour over meat, coating evenly with the marinade. Set aside for 15 minutes.

Preheat the grill to medium-high; place tenderloins on grill. Cook, turning frequently and brushing with marinade until the meat is done, about 10 to 12 minutes. Allow meat to rest a few minutes before slicing. Top the pork slices with a few spoonfuls of Pineapple Salsa.

pork loin with grapes

1 tablespoon finely chopped fresh thyme plus 6 whole sprigs

1 tablespoon finely chopped fresh parsley

1½ teaspoons finely chopped fresh rosemary plus 3 whole sprigs

1½ teaspoons finely chopped fresh sage plus 3 whole sprigs

½ cup Dijon mustard

6 tablespoons olive oil, divided

½ teaspoon kosher salt

⅛ teaspoon freshly ground black pepper

1 (3 pound) center-cut boneless pork loin, tied

1 pound fingerling or small red potatoes, halved lengthwise

6 shallots, peeled and halved through the root

1 pound red seedless grapes, snipped into 6 bunches

6 tablespoons butter, cut into ½-inch pieces

Kosher salt and freshly ground black pepper to taste

½ cup port

½ cup chicken stock

GARNISH: Sprigs of thyme, rosemary and sage

In a shallow pan large enough to hold the pork, whisk together the chopped thyme, parsley, rosemary, sage, mustard, 2 tablespoons olive oil, salt and pepper. Add pork and coat with the marinade. Cover and refrigerate at least 4 hours, turning pork after 2 hours. One hour before cooking, bring the pork to room temperature. Scrape off and reserve the marinade. Season the meat with salt and pepper.

Preheat oven to 325° and place a roasting pan in the oven to heat. In a large bowl, toss together the potatoes, shallots and grapes with 2 tablespoons of oil. Season with salt and pepper. Set aside.

Place a large sauté pan over high heat. Add 2 tablespoons of oil and heat until smoking. Add the pork and sear about 4 minutes on each side until well browned. Transfer the pork, fat-side down, to the hot roasting pan. Rub the reserved marinade over the pork and top with 3 tablespoons of the butter and the whole herb sprigs. Place the pan in the oven and roast the meat for 15 minutes. Add the reserved potato mixture around the meat. Continue roasting pork for 1 hour or until internal temperature reaches 125°.

Wipe out the sauté pan and heat over medium-high heat. Add the port and bring to a boil, scraping the bottom of the pan. When nearly evaporated, add the chicken stock and return to a boil. Whisk in the remaining 3 tablespoons of butter and season with salt and pepper. Strain through a sieve into a serving bowl and keep warm.

Transfer the pork to a cutting board and let rest, covered lightly with foil, for 10 minutes before slicing. Transfer pork slices to a warm platter and surround with potatoes, grapes and shallots. Garnish with herb sprigs and accompany with the sauce.

sugar and spice pork chops

Serves 4

4 pork chops, 1½-inches thick

4 tablespoons brown sugar

4 tablespoons chili sauce

1 teaspoon Worcestershire sauce

4 lemon slices

NOTE:
FOR FAMILY OR GUESTS, THIS IS
A QUICK AND EASY DISH.

Preheat oven to 350°. Place chops in an oiled baking dish. Combine brown sugar, chili sauce and Worcestershire. Spread mixture thickly over top of chops and place one lemon slice on each chop. Bake uncovered for 60 minutes.

tropical ribs

Barbecue Rub

4 tablespoons kosher salt

2 teaspoons freshly ground black pepper

2 teaspoons dried thyme

2 teaspoons smoked paprika

2 teaspoons chili powder

2 teaspoons sugar

2 teaspoons celery seed

1 teaspoon mustard seed

1 teaspoon dry mustard

1 teaspoon ground cumin

1 teaspoon ground or bruised fennel seeds (optional)

Ribs

3 pounds pork loin back ribs, membrane removed and
   cut into individual servings, about 3 ribs each

Barbecue Rub to taste

½ cup dark brown sugar

1 cup ketchup

¼ cup soy sauce

1 cup apricot nectar

1 cup pineapple tidbits

Combine all ingredients for barbeque rub and set aside.

Place ribs in a rectangular baking dish. Sprinkle with Barbecue Rub, to taste, and with brown sugar. Combine ketchup, soy sauce and apricot nectar. Pour over ribs.

Preheat oven to 450°. Put ribs in oven and reduce temperature to 350°. Bake 1½ to 2 hours, turning the ribs several times. Add pineapple 30 minutes before removing from oven.

kid-friendly

rosemary lamb chops

3 cloves garlic, minced

3 anchovy fillets, minced

2 tablespoons fresh rosemary, minced

¼ cup fresh parsley, minced

½ teaspoon dried thyme

½ teaspoon kosher salt

1 teaspoon freshly ground black pepper

3 tablespoons olive oil

2 tablespoons dry red wine

8 thick lamb loin chops, fat trimmed

GARNISH: 8 fresh rosemary sprigs

VARIATION:

INSTEAD OF USING THICK LAMB CHOPS, CUT SINGLE RIB CHOPS, "LOLLIPOPS", FROM A RACK; MARINATE THEM AS DESCRIBED AND COOK FOR ABOUT 4 MINUTES EACH SIDE. SERVE 3 TO 4 CHOPS PER PERSON AS AN ENTRÉE. YUMMY FINGER FOOD!

Mix together the garlic, anchovies, rosemary, parsley, thyme, salt, pepper, olive oil and wine.

Using a small sharp knife, make several shallow incisions in both sides of each lamb chop. Rub the marinade generously over both sides of the lamb chops and press it into the incisions. Place the chops on a platter and let marinate at room temperature for 1 to 1½ hours.

Heat a grill, broiler or grill pan and grill the chops 5 to 6 minutes on each side for medium-rare meat. Serve with Mint Aïoli

mint aïoli

¼ cup julienned fresh mint

1 large garlic clove, minced

1 cup mayonnaise

¼ cup extra virgin olive oil

1 tablespoon fresh lemon juice

Kosher salt and freshly ground black pepper to taste

Place the mint and garlic in the bowl of a food processor and pulse to purée. Add the mayonnaise and process until smooth. With the processor running, gradually add the olive oil and process until emulsified. Transfer the aïoli to a bowl, stir in the lemon juice, and season with salt and pepper. Refrigerate until ready to use.

festive lamb with chèvre pesto

Serves 6

8 ounces chèvre cheese

½ cup pine nuts or walnuts, toasted

½ cup fresh parsley, minced

3 garlic cloves, minced

½ cup walnut oil or olive oil

4 tablespoons fresh lemon juice

6 racks of lamb, 4 ribs to a rack

1 cup fresh bread crumbs

Preheat oven to 400°. To make pesto, pulse cheese, nuts, parsley and garlic in the bowl of a food processor. Gradually add oil and lemon juice; process until thick. Spread pesto over meat. Press bread crumbs on pesto to coat meat completely.

Place lamb, meat side up, in a roasting pan. Roast for 25 to 30 minutes or until thermometer inserted in thickest portion of meat (not touching bone) registers 125 degrees for rare. Let stand 10 minutes. Cut into each rack keeping the 4 chops slightly together.

Serve with Cherry Tomato Confit (see page 120) or Mint Aïoli (see page 135).

NOTE:

FRENCH FOR "GOAT," CHÈVRE IS A PURE WHITE GOAT'S-MILK CHEESE WITH A DELIGHTFULLY TART FLAVOR THAT EASILY DISTINGUISHES IT FROM OTHER CHEESES. STORE TIGHTLY WRAPPED IN THE REFRIGERATOR FOR UP TO 2 WEEKS.

There is a local legend from the thirties about a shelling competition for finding the rare Junonia. Supposedly, two women were walking north early one morning after a storm, and a lone determined man was walking south in the same path. As they approached one another, about equidistant between them, there appeared to be a perfect Junonia. In a last ditch, desperate attempt to grasp the prize shell, the intrepid hunter dropped his bathing suit to his feet. The horrified women turned and ran, leaving the Junonia for his easy picking.

butterflied leg of lamb with spicy herb marinade

1 leg of lamb, 8 to 9 pounds, butterflied

Kosher salt and freshly ground black pepper to taste

¼ cup olive oil

1 cup dry red wine

2 tablespoons Dijon mustard

1 teaspoon fennel seeds (optional)

2 tablespoons chopped garlic

4 sprigs fresh thyme or 2 teaspoons dried

2 teaspoons ground cumin

1 bay leaf

Lay the lamb out flat and sprinkle it on all sides with salt and a generous amount of pepper. For the marinade, combine in a bowl the olive oil, red wine, Dijon mustard, fennel seeds (optional), garlic, thyme, cumin and bay leaf; blend well.

Put the lamb in an oversized zip-top plastic bag large enough to hold it flat in one layer. Pour the marinade over the meat; turn and rub the lamb so it is evenly coated. Marinate for several hours or refrigerate overnight. Let lamb return to room temperature before cooking.

Preheat the grill to medium-high. Remove the lamb from the bag. Place lamb on the grill fat-side down and cook for 10 minutes. Turn and cook 10 minutes more for rare meat; for medium or well done, cook longer according to taste. (Time may vary depending on the temperature of the grill.) Let lamb rest for 5 minutes before serving.

curried lamb shanks

4 large lamb shanks

Freshly ground black pepper to taste

½ cup flour

2 tablespoons Madras curry powder

1½ teaspoons Anaheim chili powder

1 tablespoon fennel seeds, coarsely ground

1 tablespoon coriander seeds, coarsely ground

Canola oil for searing

1 chopped onion

1 chopped celery rib

1 large chopped carrot

1 tablespoon minced garlic

1 tablespoon minced fresh ginger

1½ cups red wine

1 bunch fresh thyme, leaves picked and chopped

½ cup low-sodium soy sauce

1 chopped banana

2 kaffir lime leaves (or finish sauce with fresh lime juice)

½ jalapeño pepper, seeds removed and chopped

Low-sodium chicken stock

Kosher salt and freshly ground black pepper to taste

COMPLIMENTS OF:

CHEF JIMMY SEARLE

BOCA BAY PASS CLUB

BOCA GRANDE, FLORIDA

Preheat oven to 325°. To prepare the shanks, season them well with black pepper. Mix flour with curry, chili powder, fennel and coriander. Completely coat shanks in this mixture.

In a large skillet coated with oil, sear shanks until brown on all sides. Remove shanks to a Dutch oven just large enough to hold them. Wipe out the skillet. Sauté onion, celery, carrot, garlic and ginger until soft, adding a small amount of oil if necessary. Deglaze pan with red wine and reduce by half. Add the thyme, soy sauce, banana, lime leaves and chili. Add shanks and completely cover with stock. Cover tightly with the lid. Braise in the oven until the meat is ready to fall off the bone, about 1½ to 2 hours.

Remove lamb from pan and reduce sauce until thickened slightly. Remove lime leaves. Purée sauce, if desired, and adjust the seasoning. (If you do not use lime leaves, add fresh lime juice to taste.)

tuscan lamb shanks with white beans

2 lamb shanks

½ teaspoon kosher salt

¼ teaspoon freshly ground black pepper

2 tablespoons olive oil

1 large onion, chopped

2 carrots, chopped

2 celery ribs, chopped

3 garlic cloves, thinly sliced

1 (14-ounce) can diced tomatoes, undrained

2 rosemary sprigs

1 cup dried navy beans, rinsed

3½ cups water

Kosher salt and freshly ground black pepper to taste

Preheat oven to 350°. Pat lamb shanks dry with paper towels and season with $^1/_2$ teaspoon salt and $^1/_4$ teaspoon pepper. Heat oil in a large heavy pan until it simmers; brown shanks well on all sides and transfer to a plate. Add onion, carrots, celery and garlic to the pan. Sauté until golden brown, about 6 minutes. Add tomatoes with juice and rosemary. Cook, stirring about 1 minute. Stir in beans, water, salt and pepper to taste. Return lamb shanks to pan and bring to a boil. Cover and braise in oven for $1^3/_4$ to 2 hours, until beans are cooked and lamb is coming off the bone; add additional water if needed. Discard rosemary and serve the shanks in flat soup bowls on top of beans.

lamb stew with polenta

Lamb Stew

4 tablespoons olive oil, divided

4 pounds lamb shoulder, deboned and cut into 1-inch cubes

Kosher salt and freshly ground black pepper to taste

1 large onion, cut into ½-inch wedges

3 small carrots, peeled and cut into ½-inch slices

4 small turnips, peeled and cut in half

1 small celery root, peeled and diced into ½-inch pieces

1 medium fennel bulb, trimmed and cut into 6 wedges

5 garlic cloves, coarsely chopped

3 teaspoons chopped fresh rosemary

2 (3-inch) cinnamon sticks

4 tablespoons flour

2 tablespoons tomato paste

Juice of one orange

½ cup dry white wine

6 cups water or chicken stock

½ teaspoon grated orange zest

4 plum tomatoes, seeded and diced into ½-inch pieces

Kosher salt and freshly ground black pepper to taste

Polenta

4 cups milk

2 cups chicken stock

1 teaspoon kosher salt

2 cups quick cooking polenta

2 tablespoons butter

3 tablespoons grated Parmesan cheese

Preheat oven to 300°. Heat 2 tablespoons olive oil in a wide, heavy pot over high heat. Season the lamb with salt and pepper and brown it on all sides, about 10 to 15 minutes. Remove the lamb and set aside.

To the hot pot, add remaining olive oil, onion, carrots, turnips, celery root, fennel, garlic, rosemary and cinnamon sticks. Stir gently for about 6 to 8 minutes. Add salt, pepper and the lamb. Sauté for another 6 to 8 minutes, adding a bit of olive oil if necessary.

Sprinkle the flour over the lamb mixture, stir and cook for about 5 minutes. Add the tomato paste and blend in thoroughly. Add the orange juice and white wine and let it reduce for a few minutes. Add water or chicken stock until it almost covers the lamb and vegetables; stir well and bring to a boil. Add the orange zest and tomatoes, cover and bake in the oven for 1 to 1¼ hours. Keep warm until ready to serve, or let cool. Refrigerate and reheat the next day. Serve stew over polenta.

To make the polenta, bring milk, chicken stock and salt to a boil. Slowly add the polenta in a steady stream; stir well and lower the heat to simmer gently until it's cooked, according to package directions. If mixture gets too thick, add more chicken stock. When polenta is done, add butter and Parmesan cheese. Adjust seasonings.

special day veal chops

Serves 4

2 tablespoons olive oil

1½ tablespoons soy sauce

1½ tablespoons whole grain Dijon mustard

1½ tablespoons sherry

1 tablespoon miso

2 green onions, minced

5 black or green peppercorns, crushed

2 garlic cloves, minced

4 bone-in veal chops, at least 1-inch thick

Combine the olive oil, soy sauce, mustard, sherry, miso, green onions, crushed peppercorns and garlic; marinate chops for at least 2 hours. Depending on thickness of chops, grill 6 to 8 minutes a side or until meat thermometer registers 130° in the center. Let rest 5 minutes before serving.

NOTE:

MISO, ALSO CALLED BEAN PASTE, IS A CULINARY MAINSTAY IN JAPANESE CUISINE. THE PEANUT BUTTER-LIKE PASTE COMES IN A VARIETY OF COLORS. THE LIGHTER-COLORED VERSIONS ARE USED IN DELICATE SOUPS AND SAUCES, MARINADES, DIPS, DRESSINGS AND AS A TABLE CONDIMENT. MISO IS EXTREMELY NUTRITIOUS, HAVING RICH AMOUNTS OF B VITAMINS AND PROTEINS.

veal alla romana

Serves 4

4 (5-ounce) thinly sliced veal cutlets

4 thin slices prosciutto

8 fresh sage leaves

¾ cup flour, for dredging

Kosher salt and freshly ground black pepper to taste

2 tablespoons olive oil

2 tablespoons butter, divided

2 tablespoons dry white wine

¼ cup chicken stock

GARNISH: Sage leaves

> **Lemon wedges**

Put the veal cutlets side by side on a sheet of plastic wrap. Lay a piece of prosciutto on top of each cutlet and cover with another piece of plastic. Gently flatten the cutlets with a rolling pin or meat mallet, until the pieces are about $1/4$-inch thick and the prosciutto has adhered to the veal. Remove the plastic and lay a couple of sage leaves in the center of each cutlet. Weave a toothpick in and out of the veal to secure the prosciutto and sage.

Put the flour in a shallow platter and season with salt and pepper. Mix with your fingers to incorporate the seasoning. Dredge the veal in the seasoned flour and shake off the excess.

Heat the oil and 1 tablespoon of butter in a large skillet over medium heat. When the butter stops foaming, put the veal in the pan, prosciutto side down, and cook for 3 minutes or until crisp. Turn the veal over and sauté the other side for 2 minutes, or until golden. Transfer the veal to a serving platter and remove the toothpicks. Keep warm while you make a quick pan sauce.

Add wine to the skillet; bring to a boil, stirring to scrape up the browned bits. Let the wine cook down for a minute to burn off some of the alcohol. Add the chicken stock and the remaining tablespoon of butter; swirl the pan around to emulsify. Season with salt and pepper. Pour the sauce over the meat; garnish with sage leaves and lemon wedges. Serve immediately.

veal chops and buttery garlic sauce

Serves 4

4 (¾-inch) thick veal chops

½ cup canola oil

½ cup flour

Kosher salt and freshly ground black pepper to taste

4 tablespoons butter

1 teaspoon chopped garlic

2 flat anchovy fillets, finely chopped

2 tablespoons minced fresh parsley

In a skillet large enough to hold the chops in one layer, heat the oil until it is hot but not smoking. Pat the chops dry with paper towels and dredge in the flour. Slip the chops into the skillet and cook over moderately high heat, turning for 8 to 10 minutes, or until they are light brown on the outside but still rosy pink within. Sprinkle the chops with salt and pepper, turn them quickly once or twice, and keep warm.

In a small saucepan, cook the butter and garlic over moderate heat until garlic turns pale gold, being careful not to brown. Add the anchovies and the parsley and cook the mixture, stirring and mashing the anchovies with a spoon, for 30 seconds. Spoon the sauce over the chops and serve immediately.

It is said that the character of Gasparilla Island was forever changed when the railroad made its last trip in 1979. The phosphate barons apparently decided that it was more economical to use the port of Tampa. Witnesses reported that the whole town came out to wave goodbye, and the engineer cried right along with everyone else. The original railroad station was turned into boutiques and an ice-cream parlor/restaurant called the Loose Caboose. The land where the tracks traversed the island was given to the Gasparilla Island Conservation and Improvement Association (G.I.C.I.A.) by the Sharp family and it was immediately converted into ideal bicycle, skating, and walking paths.

poultry

crusty chicken with creamy sage sauce

Chicken

4 (6 to 8-ounce) chicken thighs, boneless and skinless

1 egg white

1 teaspoon cornstarch

½ teaspoon fresh lemon juice

Crusting Mixture

1 cup panko crumbs or coarse breadcrumbs (ciabatta bread is ideal), dried on a baking sheet in a 200° oven for 10 minutes

1 tablespoon chopped fresh parsley

1 teaspoon kosher salt

¼ teaspoon freshly ground black pepper

Zest of 1 lemon

3 tablespoons olive oil for sautéing chicken

Lightly pound the chicken thighs between sheets of plastic wrap to an even ½-inch thickness. Blend the egg white, cornstarch and lemon juice with a fork in a wide, shallow dish; set aside.

For the crusting mixture, combine crumbs, parsley, salt, pepper and zest in another wide, shallow dish.

Dip the chicken in the egg white mixture and then in the crusting mixture. Because the crumbs are fairly coarse, they won't adhere well. Add more crumbs and pat to cover as well as possible. Transfer the chicken to a rack set over a baking sheet and air-dry chicken 20 to 30 minutes.

Preheat oven to 450°. In a large nonstick, ovenproof skillet, heat the olive oil over medium-high heat. Sauté the chicken for about 3 minutes, or until golden brown and crisp. Carefully turn with a spatula and transfer the skillet to the oven to finish cooking. Roast until just done, about 8 to 10 minutes. Do not overcook. Serve with Creamy Sage Sauce.

Creamy Sage Sauce

1 tablespoon butter

3 tablespoons minced green onions

½ cup dry white wine

½ cup heavy cream or half & half

½ cup low-sodium chicken stock

1 teaspoon fresh lemon juice

2 teaspoons minced fresh sage

Kosher salt and white pepper to taste

In a small skillet, over medium heat, melt butter and sauté green onions just until soft, 2 to 3 minutes. Add wine, cream, stock and lemon juice. If sauce looks curdled, whisk briskly. Simmer until reduced by half, whisking frequently. Add sage, salt and pepper. Set aside and keep warm in a water bath until ready to serve.

mixed up chicks

Serves 4 to 6

4 to 6 boneless, skinless chicken breast cutlets

6 tablespoons prepared pesto

5 ounces Boursin cheese

8 to 12 thin slices prosciutto

2 to 3 tablespoons olive oil

Juice of 1 lemon

1 to 2 lemons cut into wedges

Freshly ground black pepper to taste

Handful of fresh basil leaves

Cherry Tomato Confit (see page 120)

Preheat oven to 375°. Slice chicken breasts lengthwise almost all the way through. Open like a book. Spread insides of half the chicken breasts with 1 tablespoon pesto and the other half with 1 tablespoon cheese. Close them up and wrap 2 prosciutto slices around each one. Place in a baking dish. Drizzle with olive oil and lemon juice. Add lemon wedges to the pan. Season with salt and pepper and scatter basil leaves over the top. Bake for 30 minutes. Serve with Cherry Tomato Confit.

pan-roasted chicken
with lemon, olives and rosemary

1 (3-pound) chicken, cut into 8 pieces or
    3 pounds thighs and breasts, with bones

½ cup flour

2 tablespoons olive oil

2 garlic cloves, thinly sliced

2 shallots, thinly sliced

3 cups chicken stock

1 cup dry white wine

1 tablespoon grated lemon zest

3 tablespoons chopped fresh rosemary

Kosher salt and freshly ground black pepper to taste

1 cup pitted green olives, cut in half

1 tablespoon capers (optional)

1 cup cherry tomatoes, cut in half (optional)

Dredge the chicken in flour and set aside. In a large sauté pan, heat oil over high heat and cook the chicken until crisp and brown, 2 to 3 minutes on each side. Add the garlic, shallots, stock, wine, lemon zest, rosemary, salt and pepper and bring to a boil. Reduce heat, cover, and simmer for 30 minutes. Add the olives and simmer uncovered for 20 to 30 minutes, or until the chicken is cooked through and the sauce has slightly thickened. Add capers and tomatoes, if desired. Adjust seasonings and serve.

grilled chicken beachside with mango salsa

Mango Salsa

1 cup chopped fresh mango

1 cup chopped jicama

Juice of 6 limes

1 poblano chili pepper, charred, peeled, seeded and chopped

2 tablespoons chopped cilantro

⅛ teaspoon kosher salt

NOTE:

THIS GRILLED CHICKEN IS A
QUICK, LIGHT MEAL PERFECT
FOR A SUMMER EVENING.
THE CHICKEN IS TENDER AND
FLAVORFUL, AND VERY LOW IN
CALORIES.

Marinade and Chicken

3 garlic cloves, minced

6 tablespoons fresh lemon juice or Key lime juice

¾ cup olive oil

½ teaspoon kosher salt

¼ teaspoon white pepper

2 teaspoons dried tarragon

8 chicken breast halves, boned and skinned

For the salsa, mix mango and jicama with lime juice; add poblano chili, cilantro and salt. Chill for several hours.

For the marinade, combine the garlic, lemon juice, olive oil, salt, pepper and tarragon; whisk to blend.

To prepare the chicken, pound each breast half between sheets of plastic wrap with a meat tenderizer (or rolling pin). The object is to flatten the chicken to a uniform thickness so that it cooks quickly and evenly. The breasts should be about ¼ to ⅜-inch thick; they will become quite large. Place the paillards in a shallow glass dish and pour the marinade over them. Refrigerate, loosely covered with plastic, for 2 hours; turn the chicken occasionally.

Heat the grill or grill pan to medium-hot. Arrange the chicken paillards on the grill, spacing so that they do not touch. Grill for 2 minutes then turn the breasts and grill 1 to 2 minutes more on the other side. The secret is to not overcook the chicken. If the paillards are very thin, decrease the total cooking time to 3 minutes. Serve immediately with Mango Salsa.

coq au riesling

2 tablespoons olive oil

1 cup cubed bacon

1 leek, white part, finely sliced

1 garlic clove, finely minced

12 skinless chicken thighs or 2¾ pounds boneless, skinless chicken
    breasts

1 (750-ml) bottle Riesling wine

10 ounces cremini or white button mushrooms, sliced

3 bay leaves

Kosher salt and freshly ground black pepper to taste

¼ cup heavy cream (optional)

1 to 2 tablespoons chopped fresh dill

12 ounces noodles, cooked

CHEF TIP:

THIS STEW TASTES ITS
MELLOWEST BEST IF YOU
REFRIGERATE OVERNIGHT, AND
REHEAT THE NEXT DAY.

Heat the oil in a casserole or large wide pan and fry the bacon
until crisp. Add the sliced leek and garlic. Sauté with bacon for 1
minute. Add chicken, wine, mushrooms and bay leaves. Season
with salt and pepper and bring to a boil; cover the pan and simmer
gently for 30 to 40 minutes, stirring in the cream for the last couple of
minutes. Serve sprinkled with dill and buttered noodles on the side.

roast chicken with lemons

1 (3 to 4-pound) chicken

Kosher salt and freshly ground black pepper to taste

2 small lemons

Preheat oven to 350°. Wash the chicken in cold water, inside and
out. Let the water drain; pat the chicken dry with a paper towel.
Rub a generous amount of salt and pepper on the chicken, inside
and out. Puncture each lemon in at least 20 places, using a pick
or skewer. Place both lemons in the chicken's cavity. Close the
opening with poultry skewers. Tie the legs in their natural position
with string.

NOTE:

ROOM TEMPERATURE LEMONS
GIVE MORE JUICE. ROLL THEM
ON A BOARD TO RELEASE THE
JUICES BEFORE SQUEEZING.

Put the chicken in a roasting pan, breast side down. Place it in the
upper third of the oven. After 30 minutes, turn breast side up. Cook
for another 30 to 35 minutes, then increase the heat to 400°; cook an
additional 20 to 30 minutes.

To serve, place the whole chicken on a platter, leaving the lemons
inside until the chicken is carved and opened. The juices that run
out are perfectly delicious.

One tradition that has remained throughout the years is the annual lighting of the
town Christmas tree across the street from Hudson's Grocery store.
This tree lighting is sponsored by The Boca Grande Woman's Club. The main street is
blocked off and only pedestrians and golf carts are allowed. The local clergy
share a short service of readings and a homily. The families of fishermen, lawyers, plumbers
and bartenders stand side-by-side singing Christmas carols before a special
someone is chosen to flip the switch. To an outsider, the woebegone pine tree is slightly
lopsided and would surely go entirely unnoticed without the magic encirclement
of tiny white lights and the large figures of the Holy Family beneath. Like Quasimodo, it is a
tree that only a mother—or devoted community—could love.

smoke-roasted chicken thighs with maple barbecue sauce

Spice Rub

2 tablespoons ground coriander

2 tablespoons paprika

2 tablespoons ground cumin

2 tablespoons dark brown sugar

1 tablespoon kosher salt

2 tablespoons freshly ground black pepper

Chicken

8 bone-in chicken thighs, about 8 ounces each

Maple Barbecue Sauce

¾ cup ketchup

⅓ cup maple syrup

Juice of 1 lemon

Prepare a grill for indirect cooking. For the rub, combine the coriander, paprika, cumin, sugar, salt and pepper in a small bowl and mix well. Coat the thighs generously with the spice rub, pressing gently to be sure it adheres. Arrange them, skin-side down, on the side of the grill away from the heat, being careful none of the meat is directly over the coals. Put the lid on the grill with the vents open one-quarter of the way and cook for about 1 hour, turning the thighs over after 30 minutes. To check for doneness, cut into one of the thighs at its thickest point; there should be no redness near the bone.

While the chicken is on the grill, prepare the bbq sauce. Combine the ketchup, maple syrup and lemon juice in a small bowl and mix well. Baste the chicken with the sauce during the last 10 minutes of cooking, and serve the remaining sauce along with the smoked thighs.

The chicken can be baked at 350° for approximately 1 hour, instead of grilling.

baked chicken parmesan

Melted Butter Mixture

1½ cups butter

1 garlic clove, crushed

2 tablespoons Dijon mustard

2 teaspoons Worcestershire sauce

Breadcrumb Mixture

4½ cups fresh breadcrumbs or panko crumbs

1½ cups grated Parmesan cheese

1 teaspoon kosher salt

1 teaspoon freshly ground black pepper

⅓ cup minced parsley

Chicken

3 chickens, cut into serving-size pieces

For the butter mixture, melt butter in a saucepan and add garlic, mustard and Worcestershire; pour into a glass pie plate.

For the crumb mixture, combine the breadcrumbs, Parmesan cheese, salt, pepper and parsley; place in a glass pie plate.

Dip the chicken pieces in the melted butter mixture, then pat on the breadcrumbs. Refrigerate an hour or more so that crumbs will adhere.

Preheat oven to 350°. Put chicken pieces into a shallow roasting pan and drizzle with any leftover butter mixture. Bake 1 to 1¼ hours, basting once or twice. If desired, the pieces can be browned or crisped for a few minutes in the broiler.

NOTE:

PANKO, HAILING FROM JAPAN, IS A TYPE OF CRISP, LIGHT BREADCRUMB. THE CRUMBS ARE USED TO COAT FOODS FOR FRYING OR SAUTÉING, AS WELL AS IN RECIPES. BECAUSE IT IS COARSER THAN MOST BREADCRUMBS, PANKO CREATES A DELICIOUS CRUNCHY CRUST.

curry-in-a-hurry

2 tablespoons canola oil

3 tablespoons finely chopped green onions

3 to 4 tablespoons red or green Thai curry paste or to taste

2¼ pounds boneless, skinless chicken thighs, cut into strips about
　　1½-inches by ¾-inch

1 (14-ounce) can coconut milk

2 cups chicken stock

1 tablespoon fish sauce

1½ cups frozen peas

1½ cups frozen shelled edamame

1½ cups fresh green bean pieces

Cooked rice or noodles, to serve

GARNISH: Chopped fresh cilantro
　　　　　Lime wedges

Heat the oil in a large saucepan. Add green onions and cook, stirring for a minute or two. Add the curry paste. Add the chicken pieces and keep turning for 2 minutes; add coconut milk, stock and fish sauce and bring to a simmer. Add the peas, edamame and green beans. Simmer for 10 minutes. Serve over rice or noodles; garnish with cilantro and lime wedges.

cracker cottage chicken casserole

1 medium onion, chopped

1½ cups sliced fresh mushrooms

5 tablespoons butter, melted

3½ tablespoons flour

2 cups milk, heated

⅓ cup sherry

2 cups grated Swiss cheese

2 cups cooked linguine (al dente)

3 cups rotisserie chicken, skinned and cubed

1½ cups cubed ham

Kosher salt and freshly ground black pepper to taste

Grated Parmesan cheese

Preheat oven to 350°. Sauté onion and mushrooms in butter until soft. Blend in flour; add hot milk and stir until thickened. Add sherry and fold in Swiss cheese. Add linguine, chicken and ham. Season with salt and pepper. Pour into an oiled 9 x 13 x 2-inch glass baking dish; sprinkle with Parmesan cheese. Bake 45 minutes to 1 hour until browned and bubbly.

busy day chicken and rice

4 boneless, skinless chicken breast halves, each cut into 3 pieces

1 (6-ounce) box long-grain and wild rice mix with seasoning packet

1 (14-ounce) can low-sodium chicken stock

1 (10¾-ounce) can condensed, French onion-style soup

Preheat oven to 350°. In a deep baking dish, layer the chicken pieces, rice and seasoning. Pour the stock and soup over the chicken mixture. Cover and bake 45 minutes.

chicken tonnato

Tonnato Sauce

1 (6-ounce) can best quality Italian tuna, packed in olive oil, drained

3 flat anchovy fillets, drained

2 heaping tablespoons capers, drained

2 egg yolks

2 tablespoons fresh lemon juice

½ cup extra virgin olive oil

¾ cup canola oil

Chicken

3 whole chicken breasts, with bones

1 celery rib

1 medium onion, thinly sliced

1 bay leaf

1 teaspoon dried thyme

1 tablespoon kosher salt

Freshly ground black pepper to taste

GARNISH: Thin lemon slices

       Capers

       Niçoise olives, pitted

       Flat-leaf parsley

VARIATION:

TO CREATE A DELICIOUS COMPOSED SALAD, PLACE A LAYER OF MIXED LETTUCES IN BITE-SIZED PIECES ON A PLATTER OR IN A LARGE SHALLOW BOWL. PUT SOME TONNATO SAUCE ON THE GREENS. ARRANGE SLICED CHICKEN ON TOP. POUR ON MORE SAUCE AND GARNISH WITH GRAPE TOMATOES, KALAMATA OLIVES AND CAPERS. AROUND THE EDGE ARRANGE SMALL RED OR FINGERLING POTATOES THAT HAVE BEEN STEAMED AND TOSSED WITH OLIVE OIL.

A day in advance of serving, in the bowl of a food processor, combine the tuna, anchovies, capers, egg yolks and lemon juice. Process for a few seconds and then add the oils very slowly in a thin stream. Scrape the sides of the container several times.

In a saucepan, cover the chicken breasts with water; add celery, onion, bay leaf, thyme, salt and pepper. Bring to a boil; immediately reduce heat to simmer and cook breasts 15 minutes. Remove the pan from heat and let chicken cool in liquid. Remove the chicken from the bones and slice.

Taste the tonnato sauce for seasoning. You may wish to add more lemon juice at this point. Spread a small amount of the sauce over a platter. Layer chicken slices alternating with sauce. Top of chicken should be completely covered with the sauce. Cover loosely and refrigerate for 24 hours. Garnish with thin slices of lemon, capers, niçoise olives and parsley.

This recipe is an easy version of a classic from Northern Italy. It is usually made with veal and is also delicious made with poached turkey breast. Great for a summer lunch, supper or buffet.

roman-style chicken

Serves 6

6 boneless, skinless chicken breast halves

1 tablespoon olive oil

1 garlic clove, minced

Kosher salt and freshly ground black pepper to taste

6 thin slices Black Forest ham (or ham seasoned with rosemary)

1 (10-ounce) package fresh baby spinach

1 (8-ounce) package mushrooms, sliced

1 cup shredded cheese, Italian blend if available

Preheat oven to 350°. Flatten the breasts to a uniform thickness between 2 sheets of plastic wrap. Spray a 9 x 13 x 2-inch glass baking dish with olive oil cooking spray; drizzle in olive oil and scatter the minced garlic in the dish.

Arrange the chicken in the pan; sprinkle with salt and pepper. Cover with ham slices, and place spinach on top. Scatter mushroom slices over and top with cheese. Cover with foil. Bake 30 to 40 minutes. Drain off accumulated liquid. Brown quickly under the broiler.

marinated asian chicken and ribs

2 cups light soy sauce

3 cups dry sherry, divided

4 garlic cloves, minced

4 teaspoons minced fresh ginger

5 pounds chicken pieces, skinned if desired

**5 pounds baby back ribs, membrane removed, cut into serving
size pieces**

1 cup hoisin sauce

1 cup ketchup

½ cup packed dark brown sugar

2 garlic cloves, minced

Mix soy sauce, 2 cups sherry, garlic and ginger to make a marinade.
Marinate chicken and ribs in separate zip-top plastic bags. Chill
overnight, turning occasionally. Discard marinade. Combine 1 cup
sherry, hoisin, ketchup, brown sugar and garlic in a large glass jar to
make sauce. Shake to blend.

Grill chicken and ribs over medium-hot heat, basting with the
sauce. Place the ribs in the center of the grill and surround them
with chicken pieces. Rotate chicken as you baste to ensure that it is
evenly cooked if the heat varies. It will take about 30 minutes. Heat
remaining sauce to serve with entrée.

golden chicken nuggets

4 whole boneless, skinless chicken breasts

½ cup unseasoned fine dry breadcrumbs

½ cup grated Parmesan cheese

2 teaspoons seasoned salt

1 teaspoon dried thyme

1 teaspoon dried basil

½ cup butter, melted

Cut each breast into 1 to 1½-inch nuggets. Combine breadcrumbs, Parmesan cheese, seasoned salt, thyme and basil in a zip-top plastic bag. Dip nuggets in butter, then shake in crumb mixture. Place in single layer on baking sheets. Freeze. When frozen, transfer to another zip-top bag and return to freezer.

When ready to serve, bake desired number of nuggets at 400° for 10 minutes. It is not necessary to defrost nuggets.

There are so many physical attributes of Boca Grande:
the long, uncrowded, sandy beaches on the Gulf side, the exotic birdlife—
including an annual migration of white pelicans—and extensive fishing possibilities
on the Charlotte Harbor side, and the beautifully maintained sub-tropical
gardens that are mostly in public view. Long-time residents say that one can
often see a green flash on the horizon at sunset, an unforgettable burst
of Irish neon that lights up the sky for about two seconds. Skeptical visitors
counter that it takes a martini to see it, but many of us are witnesses
that iced tea with the right atmospheric conditions will do.

deliciously simple breast of duck

2 duck breast halves, skin scored

Kosher salt and freshly ground black pepper to taste

½ cup red wine

2 tablespoons balsamic vinegar

2 tablespoons raspberry vinegar

1 tablespoon butter

Season breast halves with salt and pepper on both sides. Put skin side down in a heavy skillet over low heat for 10 minutes. Pour off rendered fat. Turn heat to high and cook, meaty-side down for 5 minutes. Remove from pan and tightly wrap each portion in foil; let rest 15 minutes for rare or 20 minutes for medium rare. Deglaze skillet by adding wine and both vinegars; stir and simmer until reduced to about ¼ cup. Swirl in butter.

To serve, remove skin from duck. Slice thinly, on the diagonal, and fan out on a plate. Spoon hot sauce over top.

Delicious with wild rice or served on a bed of sautéed spinach topped with the hot sauce.

roasted lemon turkey breast

4 tablespoons butter

Juice of ½ lemon

½ bone-in turkey breast, about 2½ to 3 pounds, skin on

½ lemon, thinly sliced

2 to 3 sprigs fresh sage

1 tablespoon olive oil

1 heaping tablespoon fresh rosemary or 1 to 1½ teaspoons dried

Kosher salt and freshly ground black pepper to taste

Preheat oven to 350°. Melt butter in a small saucepan. Add lemon juice and set aside. Rinse turkey breast and pat dry with paper towel. Loosen skin of breast. Slide lemon slices and sage sprigs under skin. Secure skin to breast with 1 or 2 turkey skewers. Rub turkey breast all over with olive oil. Rub rosemary into oil and season turkey on all sides with salt and pepper. Place turkey in a roasting pan; cover and bake for 1¼ to 1½ hours, basting with butter-lemon mixture every 30 minutes. Roast until internal temperature reaches 160°.

Remove and discard skin, sage and lemon slices. Carve turkey into thin slices and serve.

"Aïoli" (see page 233) or Tonnato Sauce (see page 156) would complement the turkey.

old-fashioned turkey loaf

1½ cups chopped onion

1 tablespoon olive oil

1 teaspoon kosher salt

½ teaspoon freshly ground black pepper

½ teaspoon fresh thyme or ⅛ teaspoon dried

3 tablespoons Worcestershire sauce

6 tablespoons chicken stock

1 teaspoon tomato paste

2½ pounds ground turkey breast

¾ cup plain dry breadcrumbs

2 eggs, beaten

6 tablespoons ketchup

NOTE:

TOMATO PASTE CONSISTS OF
TOMATOES THAT HAVE BEEN
COOKED FOR SEVERAL HOURS,
STRAINED AND REDUCED TO A
DEEP RED, RICHLY FLAVORED
CONCENTRATE. TO AVOID
WASTE, FOR SMALL AMOUNTS,
PURCHASE TOMATO PASTE IN
A TUBE. KEEP REFRIGERATED
AFTER OPENING.

Preheat over to 325°. Sauté onions in oil with salt, pepper and thyme until onions are soft and translucent, approximately 15 minutes on medium-low heat. Do not brown. Add Worcestershire sauce, stock and tomato paste; mix well. Cool to room temperature.

Combine the ground turkey, breadcrumbs, eggs and onion mixture. Mix well and shape into a loaf in a 9 x 13 x 2-inch glass baking dish. Spread the ketchup on top. Bake 1 to 1¼ hours or until internal temperature reaches 160°.

turkey chili

3 tablespoons olive oil

2 onions, chopped

8 garlic cloves, chopped and divided

4 tablespoons cumin

5 tablespoons chili powder or to taste

Red pepper flakes to taste

4 pounds ground turkey

2 cups chicken stock

1 (28-ounce) can peeled and diced tomatoes

1 (12-ounce) jar salsa verde

1½ tablespoons oregano

1 bay leaf

1 green bell pepper, seeded and chopped

2 to 3 tablespoons grits or cornmeal

2 cups chopped cilantro

Heat oil in a pan; add the onions and 6 of the chopped garlic cloves. Sauté until translucent. Add the cumin, chili powder and red pepper flakes; cook an additional 2 minutes. Add the turkey, sauté until just cooked through, stirring to remove the lumps. Add the stock, tomatoes, salsa verde, oregano and bay leaf. Cook partially covered for 1 hour, adding water if necessary to keep the chili covered with liquid. Add the chopped bell pepper and the grits; cook for 30 minutes and add the balance of the garlic and the cilantro. Cook for an additional 3 to 5 minutes.

Canned beans can be added, if desired.

fish & shellfish

pompano with crispy caper sauce

Fish

2 tablespoons butter, melted

2 tablespoons fresh lemon juice

Kosher salt and freshly ground black pepper to taste

2 pounds fresh pompano, bass or halibut fillets

Crispy Caper Sauce

2 tablespoons butter

2 tablespoons olive oil

2 tablespoons small capers, rinsed, drained and dried on a paper
    towel

2 tablespoons fresh lemon juice

¼ cup fresh flat-leaf parsley, minced

Kosher salt and freshly ground black pepper to taste

Combine the melted butter, lemon juice, salt and pepper; brush
the mixture lightly over the fish fillets. Grill over medium-high heat or
in a lightly oiled grill pan. Cook 4 to 5 minutes per side until the fish
is opaque in the center and flakes easily. Arrange the fillets on a
platter.

Heat the butter and oil over medium heat in a small frying pan. Add
the capers and cook until they are just beginning to get crispy, 4 to
5 minutes. Remove from heat and stir in the lemon juice, parsley, salt
and pepper. Drizzle over the grilled fish.

damifi'll flounder

2 pounds flounder or other mild white fish

2 tablespoons fresh lemon juice

½ cup grated Parmesan cheese

4 tablespoons butter, room temperature

3 tablespoons mayonnaise

2 tablespoons chopped green onion

¼ teaspoon kosher salt

Dash of hot pepper sauce

Place fillets in single layer on a lightly oiled broiler pan. Brush with lemon juice; let stand 10 minutes. Combine Parmesan cheese, butter, mayonnaise, green onion, salt and hot pepper sauce. Place fish 4 inches from source of heat and broil 5 minutes or until fish is cooked. Remove from heat. Spread cheese mixture on top of fillets. Broil about 2 minutes or until lightly browned.

fisherman's grouper fillets

Serves 2

1 pound grouper fillets, skinned and boned

Juice of ½ lemon

1 tablespoon olive oil

1 teaspoon Dijon mustard

Kosher salt and freshly ground black pepper

¼ cup coarse dry breadcrumbs

2 tablespoons melted butter

¼ cup water or dry white wine

NOTE:

A RULE OF THUMB FOR COOKING FISH IS 8 MINUTES PER INCH OF THICKNESS.

Preheat oven to 400°. Put fillets in an oiled baking dish; sprinkle with lemon juice and brush with olive oil. Spread mustard evenly on fish. Salt to taste; grind black pepper on fish and sprinkle with bread crumbs. Drizzle with melted butter. Add water or wine to dish. Bake 15 to 20 minutes depending on thickness of fish.

thai halibut

1 teaspoon sesame oil, divided

2 teaspoons minced, peeled fresh ginger

2 garlic cloves, minced

1 cup finely chopped red bell pepper

1 cup chopped green onions

1 teaspoon curry powder

2 teaspoons red curry paste

½ teaspoon ground cumin

4 teaspoons soy sauce

1 tablespoon brown sugar

½ teaspoon salt, divided

1 (14-ounce) can light coconut milk

2 tablespoons chopped fresh cilantro

4 (6-ounce) halibut fillets

3 cups hot cooked basmati rice

4 lime wedges

VARIATION:

THIS SAUCE ALSO WORKS WELL
WITH MAHI MAHI OR CHICKEN.

NOTE:

EDAMAME IS A HEALTHY
GARNISH FOR FISH AND RICE
DISHES.

Preheat broiler. Heat ¹/₂ teaspoon sesame oil in a large nonstick skillet over medium heat. Add ginger and garlic; cook 1 minute. Add bell pepper and onions; cook 1 minute. Stir in curry powder, curry paste and cumin; cook 1 minute. Add soy sauce, sugar, ¹/₄ teaspoon salt and coconut milk; bring to simmer (do not boil). Remove from heat; stir in cilantro. Brush fish with ¹/₂ teaspoon sesame oil; sprinkle with ¹/₄ teaspoon salt. Place fish on baking sheet coated with cooking spray. Broil 7 minutes or until fish flakes easily when tested with a fork. Serve fish with sauce, rice and lime wedges.

roasted cod with garlic butter

¼ cup butter, room temperature

1½ tablespoons chopped flat-leaf parsley

1 large garlic clove, minced

2 teaspoons minced shallots

½ teaspoon Dijon mustard

1½ tablespoons minced prosciutto

1 tablespoon flour

2 tablespoons fresh lemon juice

2 tablespoons canola oil

Kosher salt and freshly ground black pepper to taste

4 (7-ounce) skinless cod fillets

GARNISH: Lemon wedges

Preheat oven to 450°. Stir together butter, parsley, garlic, shallots, mustard, prosciutto, flour, lemon juice, salt and pepper in a small bowl. Set aside.

Heat oil in a wide, deep, ovenproof skillet over medium-high heat. Season the cod fillets with salt and pepper and cook 4 minutes. Turn fillets over; cook 1 minute.

Spoon 1 tablespoon butter mixture over the top of each fillet; transfer skillet to oven and bake for 2 minutes or until fish is just cooked through and opaque in the center.

Add any remaining butter mixture to the pan and let melt, stirring with juices in pan; spoon over fish and garnish with lemons.

Serve immediately.

brown sugar chipotle salmon
with honey-berry glaze

Serves 4

1 cup raspberry or lingonberry preserves

2 tablespoons honey

2 tablespoons butter, melted

1 teaspoon fresh lime juice

1 tablespoon light brown sugar

1 tablespoon ground cumin

2 teaspoons kosher salt

1½ teaspoons chipotle powder

4 (6 to 8-ounce) salmon fillets with skin

COMPLIMENTS OF:

CATERER MEL GIONET

BOCA GRANDE, FLORIDA

Preheat oven to 425°. For the glaze, whisk together preserves, honey, butter and lime juice. Transfer 6 tablespoons glaze to a small bowl; reserve as sauce.

Place rack on rimmed baking sheet. Mix brown sugar, cumin, salt and chipotle powder on a plate. Dip flesh side of salmon in spice mixture; place coated side up on rack. Brush with remaining glaze. Bake salmon until just opaque in center, about 15 minutes. Serve, passing reserved glaze.

spa salmon

Serves 2

2 salmon fillets

½ cup white wine

2 tablespoons fresh lemon juice

Dill, fresh or dried

Preheat oven to 400°. Place fillets on a sheet of aluminum foil large enough to enclose like a package. Mix wine and lemon juice; pour wine and lemon juice over salmon fillets. Scatter dill over top. Fold and seal tightly. Place on rimmed baking sheet and bake for 20 minutes.

salmon mustard martini

Serves 4 to 6

1 cup Dijon mustard

¼ cup dry white vermouth

½ cup gin

2 tablespoons capers

1 teaspoon white pepper

1 tablespoon olive oil

1 (2 to 2½ pound) salmon fillet

10 to 12 sprigs fresh dill

Parchment paper twice as long as the fish

A day before serving, combine the mustard, vermouth, gin, capers, pepper and olive oil; chill. Spray the parchment with cooking spray. Place the fish in the middle. Coat with mustard sauce and top with dill. Make a packet; staple shut. Refrigerate for up to 8 to 24 hours. Remove from refrigerator 1 hour before cooking.

Preheat oven to 500°. Bake salmon on a rimmed baking sheet exactly 11 minutes. Paper will turn golden. Cut the packet open and serve salmon.

elegant salmon

Serves 4

4 cloves garlic, minced

2 teaspoons dried basil or 2 tablespoons fresh basil

2 tablespoons olive oil

2 tablespoons soy sauce

½ teaspoon freshly ground black pepper

1½ pounds salmon fillet, skin removed

2 tablespoons fresh lemon juice

Combine garlic, basil, olive oil, soy sauce and pepper. Place salmon in a baking dish, pour marinade over fish and refrigerate 4 hours. Add lemon juice and refrigerate 1 hour longer.

Preheat oven to 400°. Bake salmon 15 minutes (or until fish flakes and is opaque in the center). Brush twice with marinade during baking.

grilled salmon with roasted corn salad

3 cups fresh corn kernels cut from the cob or 2 (10-ounce) packages
    frozen corn, thawed and drained

1 red bell pepper, seeded and finely chopped

4 green onions, thinly sliced

½ cup chopped cilantro

1 jalapeño pepper, seeded, deveined and minced

3 tablespoons cider vinegar

1 tablespoon honey

1 tablespoon extra virgin olive oil, divided

1 teaspoon Dijon mustard

¾ teaspoon kosher salt, divided

4 (6-ounce) salmon fillets

Preheat the oven to 425°. Spray a baking sheet with nonstick spray. Spread the corn on the baking sheet. Roast, stirring occasionally, until lightly browned, about 20 minutes; cool completely.

Meanwhile, combine the bell pepper, green onions, cilantro, jalapeño pepper, vinegar, honey, 2 teaspoons of the oil, mustard and ¼ teaspoon of salt in a large bowl. Stir in the corn. Cover and chill until one hour before serving.

Rub the salmon steaks with the remaining 1 teaspoon oil and remaining ½ teaspoon salt. Heat a nonstick ridged grill pan or skillet over medium-high heat. Cook the salmon until browned on the outside and just opaque in the center, about 4 minutes on each side.

Serve with roasted corn salad.

sassy snapper with two mustards

4 (8-ounce) firm white fish fillets such as red snapper

Kosher salt and freshly ground black pepper to taste

8 ounces crème fraîche or sour cream

3 tablespoons Dijon mustard

1 tablespoon whole-grain Dijon mustard

2 tablespoons minced shallots or green onions

2 teaspoons capers, drained

1 teaspoon kosher salt

½ teaspoon freshly ground black pepper

Preheat the oven to 425°. Line a rimmed baking sheet with parchment paper. (You can also use an ovenproof baking dish.) Place the fish fillets skin side down on the pan. Sprinkle generously with salt and pepper.

Combine the crème fraîche, two mustards, shallots, capers, salt and pepper in a small bowl. Spoon the sauce evenly over the fish fillets, making sure the fish is completely covered. Bake for 8 to 10 minutes, depending on the thickness of the fish, until it's barely done. (The fish will flake easily at the thickest part when it's done.) Be sure not to overcook it. Serve with the sauce from the pan spooned over the top.

red snapper with shiitake sauce

1 pound shiitake mushrooms, sliced

1 cup chopped green onions

2 tablespoons sesame oil

¼ cup soy sauce

2 cups clam juice

Freshly ground black pepper to taste

6 tablespoons canola or peanut oil

4 tablespoons butter

6 (8-ounce) red snapper fillets

GARNISH: Lemon wedges

CHEF TIP:

THIS SHIITAKE SAUCE IS NOT
THICK. IT IS NICE TO SERVE
THE FISH IN SOUP PLATES WITH
WHITE RICE THAT HAS BEEN
COOKED IN CHICKEN STOCK.

Sauté mushrooms and green onions in sesame oil for 3 to 4 minutes over medium heat. Add soy sauce and clam juice. Bring to a boil, reduce heat and simmer for 5 minutes. Add pepper to taste. Keep on low heat while preparing fillets.

Place canola oil and butter in a large pan over medium-high heat. When butter is bubbling, add fillets, skin side down. Sauté about 5 minutes on each side. Remove from heat and place fillets on a large serving platter. Top with shiitake sauce. Garnish with lemon wedges.

pepper-crusted grilled swordfish with smoked salmon butter

Smoked Salmon Butter

½ cup butter, room temperature

2 ounces smoked salmon, roughly chopped

2 tablespoons fresh lemon juice

5 dashes red pepper sauce

3 tablespoons minced fresh chives

Kosher salt and freshly ground black pepper to taste

Fish

4 (8-ounce) swordfish steaks, about 1-inch thick

2 tablespoons olive oil

1 tablespoon kosher salt

3 tablespoons freshly ground black pepper

In a food processor, combine the butter, salmon, lemon juice and red pepper sauce; blend until smooth. Add the chives, salt and pepper; pulse a few times to incorporate the ingredients. Refrigerate or leave at room temperature if using within the hour.

Rub the fish with the oil and coat generously with the salt and pepper, pressing so it adheres. Grill on medium-high or in a grill pan until the steaks are just opaque throughout, 5 minutes per side. When done, arrange the steaks on a platter and top each with some Smoked Salmon Butter. Serve at once.

calypso swordfish

Serves 6

Mango Salsa

2 small tomatoes, cored and diced

½ medium red or yellow bell pepper, stemmed, seeded and diced

2 green onions, trimmed and minced

½ medium red onion, diced

1 ripe mango, peeled, pitted and diced

¼ cup chopped fresh cilantro

¼ cup chopped fresh flat-leaf parsley

1 tablespoon fresh orange juice

1 tablespoon fresh lime juice

Pinch of red pepper flakes

Kosher salt and freshly ground black pepper to taste

VARIATION:

TOMATOES CAN BE OMITTED FROM THE SALSA AND 1 CUP DICED FRESH PINEAPPLE SUBSTITUTED. DICED JICAMA WILL ADD CRUNCH TO THE SALSA.

Swordfish

6 (6-ounce) swordfish steaks, about 1-inch thick

Olive oil for brushing

Kosher salt and freshly ground black pepper

To make the mango salsa, combine the tomatoes, bell pepper, green onions, red onion, mango, cilantro, parsley, orange juice, lime juice, red pepper flakes, salt and pepper to taste in a large bowl and mix well. Adjust the seasonings. The salsa will keep, covered, in the refrigerator for up to 3 days.

To prepare swordfish, preheat a grill or grill pan. Brush the fish lightly with olive oil and sprinkle with salt and pepper to taste. Grill on medium-high or in a grill pan until it is opaque throughout, 5 minutes per side. Spoon a generous portion of the salsa over each steak and serve at once.

tuna with 7 spices and ponzu sauce

Spiced Tuna

¼ cup white sesame seeds, toasted

2 tablespoons black sesame seeds, toasted

2 tablespoons orange zest

1 tablespoon red pepper flakes

1 tablespoon Szechuan peppercorns, cracked

1½ teaspoons kosher salt

2 tablespoons poppy seeds

8 (6-ounce) tuna steaks

COMPLIMENTS OF:

CHEF FRANK COLTON

EAGLE GRILL

BOCA GRANDE, FLORIDA

Ponzu Sauce

1 cup pineapple juice

1 cup fresh orange juice

½ cup fresh lime juice

½ cup fresh lemon juice

1 cup mirin

1 tablespoon fresh minced ginger

1 cup soy sauce

1 cup Asian sweet chili sauce

½ cup rice wine vinegar

For the spice rub, mix together sesame seeds, orange zest, red pepper flakes, Szechuan peppercorns, salt and poppy seeds. Rub the spices liberally on the tuna steaks and grill over hot fire 2 minutes per side or to desired doneness.

For the sauce, combine the juices, mirin and ginger. On medium-low heat, reduce the mixture slowly by half. You should have about 2 cups. Add the soy sauce, chili sauce and vinegar. Simmer 5 minutes, strain and serve the sauce on the grilled tuna.

sicilian wrapped tuna

4 tuna steaks, no thicker than ½-inch (about 1½ pounds)

1 lemon, cut in half

2 teaspoons kosher salt

4 tablespoons capers, drained and rinsed

15 large sprigs flat-leaf parsley, leaves only

2 basil leaves

1 garlic clove, peeled

4 tablespoons olive oil, divided

Kosher salt and freshly ground black pepper to taste

1 large tomato

GARNISH: Fresh basil

Fresh parsley

Place tuna in a bowl of cold water with the cut lemon and 2 teaspoons kosher salt for ½ hour.

Preheat the oven to 400°. Finely chop the capers, parsley, basil and garlic. Put in a small bowl and mix with 2 tablespoons olive oil, salt and pepper. Mix well.

Drain and rinse the tuna under cold running water and dry with paper towels. Spread the caper paste over the tuna on one side. Thinly slice the tomato. Heat the remaining 2 tablespoons olive oil in a skillet and sauté the tomato for 2 minutes. Set aside.

Prepare 4 pieces of foil large enough to enclose the individual steaks. Lightly oil the shiny side before placing tuna on it. Transfer the steaks to the foil; ladle some of the tomatoes with their juices over each steak. Fold over the foil to form a package; place on baking sheet and bake 5 to 8 minutes. Open the packets, slide the fish onto each plate and serve hot with the juices poured over the tuna steaks. Sprinkle with basil and parsley.

baked tomato-basil haddock fillets

4 medium tomatoes, sliced

½ teaspoon dried basil or 2 teaspoons chopped fresh basil

1 garlic clove, minced

½ cup breadcrumbs

6 (6-ounce) haddock fillets

½ teaspoon salt

½ teaspoon pepper

½ cup butter

¾ cup white wine

1 tablespoon lime juice

½ cup grated Parmesan cheese

CHEF TIP:

SERVE THE FISH WITH LINGUINE
AS THE SAUCE IS FULL OF
FLAVOR.

Preheat oven to 400°. Place sliced tomatoes on the bottom of a
9 x 13 x 2-inch pan. Sprinkle with basil and garlic. Top with crumbs,
fillets, salt and pepper. Melt the butter; add wine and lime juice.
Pour over the fish and top with Parmesan cheese. Bake for 15 to 20
minutes.

red snapper stew with aïoli

Aïoli

3 garlic cloves

1 teaspoon kosher salt

2 egg yolks, room temperature

1½ tablespoons fresh lemon juice, room temperature

½ cup extra virgin olive oil

½ cup canola oil

NOTE:

FOR A SUCCESSFUL AÏOLI,
IT IS ESSENTIAL THAT ALL
INGREDIENTS BE AT ROOM
TEMPERATURE BEFORE
PREPARING.
LEFTOVER AÏOLI IS WONDERFUL
WITH COLD POACHED FISH,
POTATOES, GREEN BEANS,
POACHED CHICKEN OR MIXED
INTO EGG OR TUNA SALAD.

Stew

2 tablespoons olive oil

½ cup minced shallots

2 carrots, finely diced

¼ teaspoon saffron threads

1 small fennel bulb, quartered and thinly sliced

4 cups fish stock or low-sodium chicken stock

1 cup white wine

1 (3-inch) piece orange peel

2 fresh thyme sprigs

1 bay leaf

2 tomatoes, seeded and chopped

1½ pounds red snapper, cut into 1-inch strips

1 pound medium shrimp, peeled and deveined

Kosher salt and freshly ground black pepper to taste

Toasted French bread slices, about ½-inch thick

GARNISH: Chopped fennel fronds

       Orange zest

For the aïoli, place the garlic and salt on a cutting board and mince together; mash to a paste. Transfer mixture to the bowl of a food processor. Add the egg yolks and lemon juice. Process until blended. Combine olive oil and canola oil. With the processor running, start to add the oil, a drop at a time, until mixture begins to thicken (this will use about half of the oil). Very slowly, drizzle in remaining oil. You should have a thick, mayonnaise-type sauce.

Transfer the aïoli to a serving bowl and store in the refrigerator until ready to serve.

For the stew, heat the oil in a large kettle on medium heat; add the shallot, carrots, saffron and fennel. Cook, stirring, for 3 to 4 minutes. Add the stock, wine, orange peel, thyme and bay leaf. Bring to a boil. Lower heat and simmer 10 minutes. Add the tomatoes and simmer 2 more minutes.

Remove the thyme, orange peel and bay leaf; add the snapper. Simmer 3 minutes. Add the shrimp and simmer 3 more minutes. Season with salt and pepper.

To serve, place a toasted bread slice in each of 4 wide shallow soup bowls; ladle stew over bread and top with a large dollop of aïoli. Garnish with fennel fronds and orange zest.

Two of the most prominent and beloved buildings in Boca Grande are the Johann Fust Community Library (named for the 15th century German printer, who along with Gutenburg, is considered the father of printing) and Our Lady of Mercy Catholic Church. Founded by Bostonian Roger Amory, partially to house his collection of rare books and manuscripts, the Johann Fust Community Library has recently become a literary cultural center for Boca Grande. The prominent architect Burl Hoffman employed the same Spanish mission style of the library for the Catholic Church. Within the thick walls, both buildings remain remarkably cool even without air-conditioning in the oppressive heat of summer.

lobster pie

Topping

½ cup dry white breadcrumbs

¼ cup crushed potato chips

¼ cup grated Parmesan cheese

¼ teaspoon paprika

1 tablespoon dry sherry

Kosher salt to taste

Filling

1 pound cooked lobster meat (from about two 1½ pound lobsters), cut into
   bite sized pieces

2 cups clam juice, fish stock or lobster base bouillon

2 tablespoons butter

2 tablespoons flour

3 tablespoons dry sherry

½ teaspoon paprika

½ teaspoon tomato paste

½ cup heavy cream

Kosher salt and white pepper to taste

Preheat oven to 350°. For topping, combine breadcrumbs, potato chips,
Parmesan cheese, paprika, sherry and salt in a bowl. Stir well and set
aside.

Butter a 9-inch deep glass pie plate or 2 quart baking dish. Fill it with the
lobster meat.

In a large saucepan, bring the clam juice or fish stock to a boil. Pour into
a measuring cup. In the same saucepan, melt the butter, sprinkle on the
flour and cook over low heat stirring constantly for 2 minutes. Slowly whisk
in the hot clam juice or stock and whisk until mixture is smooth. Add the
sherry, paprika, tomato paste and cream. Cook, stirring constantly, until
mixture comes to a boil. Season to taste with salt and pepper. Lower the
heat; simmer for 10 minutes, stirring occasionally. Pour the cream sauce
over the lobster, and then sprinkle with the crumb topping. Bake for 25
minutes or until the sauce is bubbling at the edges. Serve hot.

lobster tails with pernod butter

Pernod Butter

8 tablespoons butter, room temperature

2 tablespoons Pernod liqueur, or to taste

2 teaspoons dried crumbled tarragon

Lobster

4 (7 to 8-ounce) rock lobster tails

Melted butter

Oil for grill

To make Pernod butter, combine butter with Pernod and tarragon. Beat until fluffy. Cover and refrigerate until ready to serve.

To prepare the lobster tails, use kitchen shears to cut the top membrane and discard. Partially loosen meat from shell with your hand, leaving tail section connected. Brush lobster tails with melted butter.

Lightly oil a grill and heat to medium-high. Arrange tails on grill, cut side down, and cook for 2 to 3 minutes. Turn tails over and continue cooking until done, 7 to 9 minutes. (Grilling lobster shell side down for most of the cooking time helps the lobster meat retain its juices.) The lobster meat is cooked when it turns opaque. The shell may char. Serve lobster tails immediately with Pernod butter; the chilled butter will melt into the grilled lobster tails.

sea scallops with capers and lemon

12 fresh sea scallops

Kosher salt and freshly ground black pepper to taste

¼ cup olive oil

3 tablespoons butter

1 tablespoon finely chopped shallots

2 tablespoons salt-packed capers, rinsed of excess salt

Juice of half a lemon

⅓ cup finely chopped flat-leaf parsley

Pat scallops dry with paper towels; season lightly with salt and pepper. Heat a large sauté pan or skillet over medium-high heat and add oil. After 30 seconds, add scallops; do not crowd pan, working in batches if necessary. Brown the scallops, about 2 minutes, then turn and cook other side, 2 or 3 minutes. When second side is dark golden, transfer scallops to a platter; cover and keep warm.

Return sauté pan to heat; add butter and cook until it begins to foam and turn golden. Add shallots and capers; sauté for 1 minute, then add lemon juice (being careful to avoid sputtering butter) and chopped parsley.

To serve, spoon butter, shallots and capers over scallops.

sea scallops with smoked chili cream

Smoked Chili Cream

2 teaspoons chipotle powder

Juice of 2 fresh limes

¾ cup sour cream

Kosher salt to taste

CHEF TIP:

THIS DELICATE SMOKED CHILI
SAUCE ADDS A ZING TO SWEET
SCALLOPS. IT'S ALSO GREAT
ON GRILLED FISH, ENCHILADAS
OR BAKED POTATOES.

Caramelized Scallops

2 pounds large sea scallops

2 tablespoons chopped fresh parsley

Kosher salt and freshly ground black pepper to taste

2 tablespoons olive oil

2 tablespoons butter

GARNISH: Sliced lemons

        Chopped chives

For smoked chili cream, mix chipotle powder in lime juice and let it
sit and "bloom" for 5 to 10 minutes; whisk mixture into sour cream.
Add salt to taste.

For scallops, on a cutting board arrange the scallops with flat side
down. Pat dry with paper towels. Sprinkle the top liberally with
parsley, salt and pepper. Heat the oil and butter in a large skillet until
oil just begins to smoke. Reduce heat to medium high and place
scallops in skillet seasoned side down. Do not disturb them for 2 to
3 minutes. This allows the naturally present sugars in the scallops to
caramelize. Turn and sear on opposite side for 1 to 3 minutes longer
depending on the size of the scallop. Top with smoked chili cream
and garnish with lemons and chives. Serve immediately.

scallops & basil mango sauce

2 ripe mangoes, peeled, seeded and chopped

2 cups fresh orange juice

½ cup chopped fresh basil

3 tablespoons canola oil

2 pounds sea scallops

Kosher salt and freshly ground black pepper to taste

GARNISH: Julienned fresh basil leaves

NOTE:

BASIL LEAVES HAVE THE BEST
FLAVOR BEFORE THE PLANT
FLOWERS.

Place the mango in a food processor and purée. There should be almost 2 cups of purée. Add the orange juice and pulse until combined. Stir in the chopped basil; set aside.

Heat oil in a large heavy skillet until it is almost smoking. Season scallops with salt and pepper and add to skillet in one layer; do not crowd. Cook for about 2 minutes, until light brown on the bottom. Turn over and cook the other side for another 2 to 3 minutes. Cooking times will vary according to the size of the scallops. When they are browned on both sides, they are ready. Remove the scallops from the pan and keep warm.

Add the mango sauce to the pan and heat for 1 minute.

To serve, place a spoonful of sauce under each scallop and sprinkle with basil leaves. Serve immediately.

boca scampi

1½ cups dry white wine

3 cups lobster stock made from lobster base bouillon

3 tablespoons lemon juice

5 tablespoons butter, divided

3 tablespoons finely minced garlic

1 large shallot, finely minced

3 teaspoons Dijon mustard

¾ teaspoon black peppercorns, coarsely cracked

Kosher salt to taste

1½ pounds shrimp, cleaned and butterflied

10 ounces linguine

6 tablespoons grated Parmesan cheese

6 tablespoons panko breadcrumbs

½ teaspoon paprika

GARNISH: Flat-leaf parsley, finely minced

To prepare the stock, in a 3 to 5 quart heavy-bottomed saucepan over moderately high heat, reduce the wine, stock and lemon juice to 1 cup. Remove from the heat and set aside.

In a skillet over medium-low heat, melt 3 tablespoons butter. Add garlic and shallots and cook until tender, 8 to 10 minutes. Add reserved wine mixture, mustard and peppercorns; cook, stirring frequently, for 4 to 6 minutes. Add salt to taste.

Preheat oven to 425°. In an 8 x 11 x 2-inch glass baking dish, arrange shrimp in 4 rows lengthwise with the tails standing up. Pour wine mixture evenly over the shrimp.

In a large pot of boiling salted water, cook linguine; drain. Add 2 tablespoons butter to keep pasta from sticking together. Combine cheese, breadcrumbs and paprika. Sprinkle over the shrimp. Bake approximately 10 minutes until the shrimp are just cooked and the crumb topping is golden brown. Serve over linguine and garnish with parsley.

shrimp & pea risotto with gremolata

Serves 4

Shrimp Stock

1 pound medium shrimp, shells on

2 cups water

1½ cups chicken broth

1 cup chopped leek greens (tops only)

9 black peppercorns

4 fresh parsley sprigs

2 bay leaves

CHEF TIP:

IF MORE STOCK IS NEEDED FOR
THIS RISOTTO, USE CHICKEN
STOCK OR CLAM JUICE.

Risotto

2 tablespoons butter

2 tablespoons olive oil

1 cup chopped leeks, white part

1 cup Arborio rice

¾ cup dry white wine

1 cup frozen peas, thawed

1 teaspoon kosher salt

¼ teaspoon cayenne pepper

¼ teaspoon ground nutmeg

2 tablespoons butter

2 tablespoons grated Parmesan cheese

GARNISH: Bacon-Chive Gremolata (see page 189)

For the stock, peel and devein the shrimp; set aside. Place shells, water, chicken broth, leek greens, peppercorns, parsley sprigs and bay leaves in a saucepan and bring to a boil. Reduce heat to medium-low and simmer stock for 10 minutes. Strain stock through a colander into a bowl; discard solids. Return stock to saucepan over low heat.

To prepare the risotto, melt butter and oil in a sauté pan over medium heat. Add chopped leeks; sauté 2 minutes, then stir in rice and sauté 2 minutes. Do not allow rice or leeks to brown. Deglaze pan with white wine, stirring frequently until liquid evaporates. Add ½ cup of warm shrimp stock and stir until absorbed. Continue to stir frequently and add stock, ½ cup at a time, until all stock is used and the rice is tender, 20 to 25 minutes. Stir in the peas and shrimp; cook until shrimp are pink and firm, about 5 minutes. Season risotto with salt, cayenne and nutmeg. Remove from heat, add butter and Parmesan cheese. Garnish with Bacon-Chive Gremolata.

bacon-chive gremolata

3 strips thick-sliced bacon, diced

2 tablespoons fresh chives, snipped

2 tablespoons fresh parsley, minced

1 tablespoon lemon zest, minced

½ teaspoon garlic, minced

Kosher salt to taste

Sauté bacon in a skillet over medium-high heat until crisp, about 5 minutes; drain and cool. Combine bacon with chives, parsley, lemon zest, garlic and salt.

This topping is delicious served over asparagus.

bourbon shrimp

¼ cup butter

1 pound shrimp, peeled and deveined

¼ cup bourbon

1 teaspoon tomato paste

¼ cup heavy cream

2 tablespoons lemon juice

⅓ cup chopped pecans (optional)

Kosher salt and freshly ground black pepper to taste

Cooked rice

GARNISH: Minced chives

In a sauté pan melt butter; add shrimp and sauté for 1 minute. Pour in bourbon and light with a match, shaking the pan until the flame dies. With a slotted spoon, remove the shrimp to a warm platter. Add the tomato paste and cream to the sauté pan. Bring the mixture to a boil and lower heat to medium. Reduce until thickened and mixture coats the back of a spoon. Add lemon juice, pecans, salt and pepper. Return shrimp to mixture and reheat. Serve over rice and sprinkle with chives.

shrimp enchiladas

2 tablespoons olive oil, divided

½ cup chopped red bell pepper

½ cup minced onion

1 jalapeño pepper, cored, seeded and minced

1 fresh green chile pepper, cored, seeded and diced

½ teaspoon minced garlic

½ teaspoon dried oregano

½ teaspoon kosher salt

Pinch freshly ground black pepper to taste

Pinch cayenne

3 tablespoons flour

3 tablespoons water

1 cup milk

1 cup grated Monterey Jack cheese, divided

¼ cup sour cream

1 pound medium shrimp, peeled and deveined

¾ cup chopped green onions, divided

2 medium tomatoes, peeled, seeded and chopped, divided

8 (8-inch) flour tortillas

GARNISH: Guacamole and salsa

Preheat oven to 350°. Oil a large baking dish. In large heavy saucepan, heat 1 tablespoon of the olive oil over medium heat. Add bell pepper, onion, jalapeño, green chile, garlic and oregano. Cook until tender, about 5 minutes, stirring occasionally. Stir in salt, pepper and cayenne.

In a small bowl, combine flour and water; whisk to blend and add to bell pepper mixture. Add milk and stir until well blended. Reduce heat and simmer until slightly thickened, stirring constantly, about 3 minutes. Add ½ cup of the Monterey Jack cheese and stir until melted. Remove from heat and stir in sour cream.

In a large skillet, heat remaining 1 tablespoon olive oil over high heat. Add shrimp and ½ cup of the green onions. Stir until shrimp just turn pink, about 2 minutes. Stir in half of the bell pepper mixture and half of the tomatoes. Remove from heat. Spoon approximately $1/2$ cup of the shrimp mixture onto 1 tortilla and roll tightly. Place, seam down, in prepared baking dish and repeat with remaining tortillas. (Can be prepared to this point up to 2 hours in advance. Cover and chill.)

Top enchiladas with remaining half of the bell pepper mixture. Cover with foil and bake 30 to 40 minutes until thoroughly heated. Top with remaining $1/2$ cup Monterey Jack cheese, $1/4$ cup green onions and remaining half of the tomatoes. Return to oven until cheese melts. Garnish with guacamole and salsa, and serve immediately.

shrimp with "pearls"

Serves 2

1 cup pearl (Israeli) couscous
1 cup sugar snap peas, strings removed, halved diagonally
3 tablespoons butter, divided
Kosher salt and freshly ground black pepper to taste
10 ounces large shrimp, peeled and deveined
$1/2$ cup dry white wine
1 tomato, seeded and finely chopped
$1/4$ teaspoon sugar
2 tablespoons chopped fresh tarragon

Cook couscous in salted boiling water, uncovered, about 7 minutes. Stir in sugar snaps and cook another 3 minutes until couscous is done. Drain and transfer to a bowl; stir in 1 tablespoon butter and salt and pepper to taste.

While couscous and sugar snaps cook, toss shrimp with salt and pepper. Heat remaining 2 tablespoons butter in a 10-inch skillet over medium high heat until foam subsides. Add shrimp and sauté, turning once, until just cooked through, about 3 minutes total. With a slotted spoon, transfer shrimp to a plate. Add wine, tomato and sugar to the skillet and cook over medium-high heat until tomato starts to fall apart, about 4 minutes. Return shrimp to skillet and stir in tarragon. Adjust seasoning. Serve shrimp with the sauce over the couscous and snap pea mixture.

shrimp with feta

2 large onions, thinly sliced

⅓ cup olive oil

4 large tomatoes, peeled, seeded and coarsely chopped or
    2 (14.5 ounce) cans of petite diced tomatoes

3 tablespoons finely chopped parsley

¼ teaspoon sugar

Kosher salt and freshly ground black pepper to taste

2 garlic cloves, minced

1 large tomato, peeled, cored and left whole

3 pounds large shrimp, peeled and deveined

¾ pound feta cheese, crumbled (do not use low-fat; it does not melt)

GARNISH: Chopped fresh parsley or dill

Preheat oven to 450°. In a large pan or a stovetop casserole with lid, sauté the onions in olive oil; add the chopped tomatoes, parsley, sugar, salt, pepper and garlic. Cover and simmer 30 minutes.

Cut an X partially through the tomato and open it slightly. Place the whole tomato in the center of the skillet. Arrange the raw shrimp in the sauce in a circular fashion dipping them down into the sauce. Crumble the cheese over the shrimp and tomato. Bake for 10 minutes. Garnish with parsley or dill.

Serve with crusty bread or spoon over penne pasta.

seafood mediterranean

3 garlic cloves, chopped

½ cup olive oil

6 lobster tails, cut in half lengthwise then in thirds crosswise

2 (14.5 ounce) cans petite cut diced tomatoes

1 cup white wine

1½ tablespoons chopped fresh oregano or 1 teaspoon dried

1½ teaspoons kosher salt

½ teaspoon freshly ground black pepper to taste

2 bay leaves

1½ dozen little neck clams

1 pound shrimp, peeled and deveined

1 cup coarsely chopped fresh parsley

NOTE:

THE MOST IMPORTANT THING TO KNOW ABOUT COOKING SHRIMP IS WHEN TO STOP THE COOKING PROCESS. SHRIMP ARE DONE WHEN THEY JUST TURN PINK. BE VIGILANT TO AVOID OVERCOOKING.

In a large covered skillet or pan, sauté the garlic in olive oil. Add the lobster pieces and sauté lightly. Add the tomatoes, wine, oregano, salt, pepper and bay leaves. Bring the mixture to a boil; reduce the temperature to a simmer.

Add the clams and cook, covered, over low heat until the clams have opened. Add the shrimp and simmer until they turn pink, 3 to 5 minutes. Discard any clams that do not open. Add parsley and serve in wide shallow soup bowls.

Serve with a green salad and lots of garlic bread to soak up the delicious broth.

palm island shrimp and grits

Shrimp and Stock

1 pound medium to large shrimp, shells on

4 tablespoons butter

¾ cup chopped onion

½ cup chopped green bell pepper

2 garlic cloves, minced

1 tablespoon flour

1 cup diced tomatoes, fresh or canned

½ teaspoon dried thyme

1 tablespoon tomato paste

½ cup heavy cream

2 teaspoons Worcestershire sauce

2 dashes red pepper sauce

Kosher salt to taste

CHEF TIP:
½ POUND SMOKED PRE-COOKED SAUSAGE, SLICED, CAN BE ADDED WITH THE SHRIMP STOCK OR CLAM JUICE.

Grits

3½ cups chicken stock or water

¾ cup old fashion grits

¼ teaspoon kosher salt

6 ounces Cheddar cheese, grated

3 tablespoons butter

GARNISH: Chopped fresh parsley

For the stock, peel and devein the shrimp; set aside. Place shells in 2 cups of water in a saucepan. Boil until liquid is reduced by half. Strain through a sieve, pressing down on the shells to extract flavor.

For the shrimp, melt butter in a large skillet over medium heat. Sauté onion, bell pepper and garlic until tender. Sprinkle with flour; whisk to combine. Cook, stirring for 3 minutes. Add tomatoes with their juice, thyme and ½ cup of the shrimp stock. Simmer 3 minutes. Add tomato paste, cream, Worcestershire sauce and hot pepper sauce. Add shrimp and more stock if necessary. Simmer 2 to 3 minutes until shrimp are cooked. Add salt to taste.

To prepare the grits, bring to a boil chicken stock or water and slowly stir in the grits. Reduce heat and cook until grits are tender and the water has been absorbed, 15 to 20 minutes. Remove from heat and add salt, cheese and butter. Stir until melted.

Place a portion of grits in the middle of each plate. Spoon shrimp over grits and garnish with parsley.

pink elephant shrimp

Serves 6

1 cup butter

4 dozen shrimp, peeled and deveined

1 teaspoon kosher salt

½ teaspoon black pepper

2 teaspoons paprika

3 teaspoons garlic salt

⅓ cup good sherry

A FAVORITE RECIPE FROM
THE GASPARILLA COOKBOOK,
CIRCA 1961.

Melt butter in skillet. Add the shrimp and seasonings; sauté about 4 minutes until shrimp are done and add sherry. Serve over toast points (or linguini) with salad and crusty bread.

zarzuela de mariscos

4 tablespoons olive oil, divided

1 pound snapper, grouper or other firm fish, skinned and cut in
   1-inch chunks

Flour

Kosher salt and freshly ground black pepper to taste

1 pound shrimp, peeled and deveined

2 tablespoons brandy

1 medium onion, chopped

2 garlic cloves, minced

1 red bell pepper, chopped

2 tomatoes, chopped (or 1 cup canned tomatoes, broken up)

½ cup dry white wine

1 (8 to 10-ounce) can whole clams, drained, liquid reserved
   (or use freshly shucked clams)

Hot cooked rice

GARNISH: Chopped parsley

NOTE:

A ZARZUELA IS A MUSICAL
COMEDY OR OLD
VAUDEVILLIAN-TYPE VARIETY
SHOW THAT IS STILL PERFORMED
IN SPAIN. THUS, THE ZARZUELA
DE MARISCOS IS A MEDLEY
OF SHRIMP, FISH, MUSSELS,
SCALLOPS, ETC. COOKED IN
EXTRA VIRGIN OLIVE OIL. IT IS
TRADITIONALLY SERVED IN A
MEDITERRANEAN CLAY POT.

In a large sauté pan on medium, heat 3 tablespoons olive oil. Lightly dust the fish chunks with a mixture of flour, salt and pepper. Sauté the fish in oil until lightly browned. Add shrimp and sauté quickly until shrimp are a light pink. Warm the brandy in a small saucepan, ignite and pour over the fish-shrimp mixture. With a slotted spoon, remove the fish and shrimp to a bowl and set aside.

Add onion, garlic and bell pepper to the pan with the remaining tablespoon of olive oil. Sauté until tender; stir in tomatoes, wine and clam liquid. Bring to a boil over high heat. Cook and stir until the liquid is slightly reduced. Lower heat; add the fish, shrimp and clams. Adjust the seasoning and cook 2 more minutes. Serve in shallow soup bowls over hot cooked rice. Garnish with chopped parsley.

creole jambalaya

3 tablespoons butter

1 pound cooked ham, cubed

5 medium onions, chopped

2 garlic cloves, minced

3 (14.5-ounce) cans petite diced tomatoes, undrained

3½ cups water, divided

1 pound smoked sausage, sliced

2 green bell peppers, chopped

1 (6-ounce) can tomato paste

¼ cup minced parsley

2 bay leaves

2 teaspoons dried tarragon

1 teaspoon dried thyme

2 teaspoons kosher salt

2 cups dry white wine

3 cups uncooked white rice

1¼ pounds shrimp, peeled and deveined

1 pound fresh scallops

Melt butter in a large deep pan. Add ham, onions and garlic. Sauté 3 to 4 minutes. Add tomatoes with liquid, 1½ cups water, sausage, green bell pepper, tomato paste, parsley, bay leaves, tarragon, thyme and salt. Cover and simmer 1½ hours. Can be made ahead to this point.

Add the wine, 2 cups water and rice. Heat to boiling; reduce heat, cover and simmer 20 minutes or until rice is tender. Add more water if necessary. During last 5 minutes, stir in shrimp and scallops.

mussels in tomato-fennel broth

2 tablespoons olive oil

1 medium onion, finely chopped

2 shallots, minced

½ medium fennel bulb, trimmed and thinly sliced

1 cup dry white wine

1 (28-ounce) can plum tomatoes, coarsely chopped

Pinch of saffron threads

Freshly ground black pepper

3 pounds mussels, beards removed and mussels scrubbed

½ cup chopped fresh flat-leaf parsley

Heat the olive oil in a large soup pot over medium heat. Add the onion, shallots and fennel; sauté until softened, 10 to 15 minutes. Add the wine and tomatoes and their juice; bring to a boil. Lower the heat and simmer, partially covered, for 15 minutes. Add the saffron and pepper to taste and simmer an additional 10 minutes. (The broth can be prepared up to this point and refrigerated for up to 1 week, or frozen for up to 1 month.)

Return the broth to a boil over high heat. Add the mussels and parsley; cover, reduce the heat to medium, and let the mussels steam until they open, about 5 minutes. (Discard any that do not open.) Spoon the mussels and broth into large soup bowls and serve with crusty bread and a salad.

fish exchange

Bass . . . . .Grouper, Halibut, Snapper, Mahi Mahi

Bluefish. .Mackerel, Kingfish

Cod. . . . . .Scrod, Lingcod, Flounder, Haddock

Flounder. . . . . .Haddock, Catfish

Grouper .Black Sea Bass, Snapper, Halibut, Tilefish

Haddock .Cod

Halibut . . . . .Grouper, Cod, Snapper

Mahi Mahi . . . . .Snapper, Salmon, Sea Trout, Cod, Cobia

Pompano. . . . . .Snapper

Salmon. . . . . .Artic Char, Sea Trout

Snapper .Grouper, Sole, Cod, Flounder, Mahi Mahi

Sole. . . . . .Flounder, Haddock, Catfish

Swordfish . . . . .Shark, Tuna, Marlin, Wahoo

Trout . . . . .Catfish, Salmon

Tuna . . . . .Swordfish, Shark, Wahoo, Amberjack

pasta,
rice & grains

fettuccine with sausage, olives and broccoli rabe

Serves 4

3 tablespoons olive oil

1 pound Italian sausage, casings removed and torn into 1-inch chunks

4 to 6 garlic cloves, minced

¼ pound broccoli rabe, cleaned and coarsely chopped

Kosher salt to taste

1 pound fettuccine (fresh or dried)

½ cup pitted kalamata olives, cut in half

¼ cup heavy cream

¼ teaspoon red pepper flakes or to taste

2 teaspoons chopped fresh oregano

Freshly ground black pepper to taste

Grated pecorino

CHEF TIP:

A COMBINATION OF SWISS CHARD AND SMALL BROCCOLI PIECES CAN BE SUBSTITUTED FOR BROCCOLI RABE.

Pour olive oil into skillet over medium heat. Cook sausage until it begins to brown, about 5 minutes. Add the garlic and cook until just fragrant and beginning to brown, about 2 minutes. Add the broccoli rabe and sauté for 3 to 4 minutes.

In a large pot of salted boiling water, cook pasta al dente, about 5 minutes for fresh fettuccine or 8 to 10 minutes for dried.

Add olives to the skillet. Sauté 1 minute; stir in the cream. Drain the pasta and transfer to a large bowl. Add the sausage mixture and toss. Add red pepper flakes, oregano, salt and pepper to taste. Toss and serve, passing grated pecorino for topping.

spaghetti with
eggplant, tomatoes and mozzarella

1 large eggplant (about 1¾-pounds), peeled and cut into ¼-inch
    cubes

¼ cup olive oil, divided

¾ teaspoon kosher salt, divided

Freshly ground black pepper to taste

1 medium onion, chopped

2 garlic cloves, minced

2 pounds tomatoes, peeled and chopped

¾ pound spaghetti

3 tablespoons fresh basil, chopped

½ pound fresh mozzarella, cut into ½-inch cubes

CHEF TIP:

BEFORE DRAINING COOKED
PASTA, ALWAYS REMOVE AND
SET ASIDE ABOUT 1 CUP OF
THE PASTA WATER. YOU CAN
ADD PASTA WATER TO SAUCE
AND PASTA MIXTURE IF IT IS
TOO DRY.

Preheat oven to 425°. Toss the eggplant with 2 tablespoons of the
oil, ¹/₄ teaspoon salt and a pinch of pepper. Spread the eggplant on
a baking sheet. Roast, stirring occasionally, until tender and brown,
about 20 minutes.

Meanwhile, heat the remaining 2 tablespoons of oil in a large skillet
over moderate heat. Add the onion; cook, stirring occasionally, until
golden brown, about 8 minutes. Stir in the garlic and cook 1 minute
more.

Add the tomatoes, ¹/₂ teaspoon salt and pepper. Increase the heat
to high. Cook, stirring occasionally until the sauce is thickened,
about 10 minutes.

In a large pot of salted boiling water, cook the spaghetti al dente,
about 12 minutes. Drain. Toss the pasta with the eggplant, tomato
sauce, basil and mozzarella. Serve at once.

pappardelle with tomatoes, arugula and parmesan

9 ounces pappardelle (wide ribbon pasta), fresh or dried

2 tablespoons olive oil

¼ teaspoon red pepper flakes

3 garlic cloves, thinly sliced

1½ cups halved yellow tear-drop cherry tomatoes

1½ cups halved grape tomatoes

3 tablespoons fresh lemon juice

1 teaspoon kosher salt

5 cups loosely packed trimmed arugula

⅓ cup grated Parmesan cheese

2 bacon slices, cooked and crumbled

CHEF TIP:

IF YELLOW CHERRY TOMATOES ARE NOT AVAILABLE, SUBSTITUTE MORE GRAPE TOMATOES.

NOTE:

PAPPARDELLE, WHICH MEANS "GULP DOWN", IS A FLAT, LONG, WIDE NOODLE WITH RIPPLED EDGES.

In a large pot of salted boiling water, cook pasta al dente. Drain and keep warm. Heat oil in a large nonstick skillet over medium heat. Add pepper flakes and garlic to skillet; cook 1 minute or until garlic is fragrant. Add tomatoes; cook just until heated, stirring gently. Remove skillet from heat; stir in lemon juice and salt. Combine the hot pasta, arugula and warm tomato mixture in a large bowl, tossing to coat. Top with cheese and bacon. Serve immediately.

pesto pine nuts

2 cups lightly toasted pine nuts

3 tablespoons homemade or store purchased pesto

1 tablespoon finely grated Parmesan cheese

1 teaspoon kosher salt

Toss pine nuts, pesto, Parmesan cheese and salt in a large bowl. Spread in a single layer on a baking sheet and let dry for at least 2 hours. Can be frozen in a zip-top bag. These nuts are a flavorful addition to pasta and salads.

plum tomatoes, artichokes and penne

Serves 6

1 (12-ounce) jar oil-marinated artichoke hearts, drained, oil reserved

1 cup chopped onion

1 tablespoon finely minced garlic

2 (28-ounce) cans plum tomatoes, crushed

2 tablespoons tomato paste

1 teaspoon dried basil

½ teaspoon dried oregano

Pinch of red pepper flakes

Kosher salt and freshly ground black pepper to taste

2 tablespoons chopped flat-leaf parsley

12 ounces penne pasta, cooked al dente

NOTE:

"AL DENTE", AN ITALIAN PHRASE THAT MEANS "TO THE TOOTH", IS THE KEY TO PERFECT PASTA. IT DESCRIBES A TEXTURE THAT OFFERS A SLIGHT RESISTANCE WHEN BITTEN INTO, WITHOUT BEING OVER COOKED AND MUSHY.

Pour 3 tablespoons reserved artichoke oil marinade into a heavy pot. Add the onions and stir over low heat for 10 minutes, adding garlic during the last 2 minutes. Stir in tomatoes, tomato paste, basil, oregano and red pepper flakes. Season with salt and pepper. Simmer, uncovered, for 45 minutes. Cut the artichokes in half lengthwise; add artichokes to the tomato mixture along with the remaining oil marinade. Simmer for 20 minutes, stirring occasionally. Stir in the parsley and adjust the seasonings. Serve in shallow bowls over cooked penne.

orzo and artichoke salad

1½ cups orzo

2 tablespoons plus 1 cup extra virgin olive oil

2 (6-ounce) jars marinated artichokes, drained and quartered

2 tablespoons white wine vinegar

1 teaspoon Dijon mustard

Kosher salt and freshly ground black pepper to taste

2 tablespoons chopped fresh basil

2 ounces prosciutto, minced

½ cup grated Parmesan cheese

2 tablespoons fresh lemon juice

¼ cup minced fresh parsley

4 green onions, minced

In a pot of salted boiling water, cook orzo for 7 to 8 minutes until al dente. Drain and refresh under cold water. In a bowl, toss orzo with 2 tablespoons olive oil. Add artichoke pieces.

In a small bowl, whisk together vinegar, mustard, salt and pepper. Add remaining olive oil in a stream, whisking until dressing is emulsified. Add basil and pour desired amount of dressing over orzo mixture. Add prosciutto, Parmesan cheese, lemon juice, parsley and green onions. Toss to combine and adjust seasoning.

island time pasta salad

½ pound orecchiette or other small pasta

2 carrots, shredded

2 cups fresh broccoli, chopped

½ fennel bulb, chopped

1 red bell pepper, seeded and finely chopped

½ cup finely chopped red onion

¼ cup flat-leaf parsley, minced

3 tablespoons olive oil

2 tablespoons nonfat plain yogurt

2 tablespoons light sour cream

4 teaspoons fresh lemon juice

½ teaspoon kosher salt

½ teaspoon freshly ground black pepper

½ pint cherry or grape tomatoes, halved

¼ cup grated Parmesan cheese

NOTE:
ORECCHIETTE, WHICH MEANS
"LITTLE EARS", IS PASTA SHAPED
LIKE TINY DISKS.

In a large pot of salted boiling water, cook pasta al dente; drain. Rinse under cold water; drain again. Place the pasta in a large bowl. Add the carrots, broccoli, fennel, bell pepper, red onion and parsley to the pasta.

Combine the olive oil, yogurt, sour cream, lemon juice, salt and pepper in a medium bowl; stir into the pasta and vegetable mixture. Stir in the tomatoes and Parmesan cheese. Serve at room temperature. Pasta can be refrigerated for up to 2 days.

shoreside mac 'n cheese with lobster

Cheese Sauce

½ cup butter

½ cup flour

4 cups milk

16 ounces extra sharp white Cheddar cheese, grated

4 ounces Parmesan cheese, grated

Kosher salt and freshly ground black pepper to taste

Pasta

6 tablespoons butter

1 medium shallot, diced

4 garlic cloves, minced

8 ounces lobster meat, cut into small pieces

1 pound cavatelli pasta, cooked al dente

¼ cup breadcrumbs

¼ cup grated Parmesan cheese

VARIATION:

IN PLACE OF LOBSTER IN THE MAC' N CHEESE, USE 6 TO 8 OUNCES EACH OF SHRIMP AND SCALLOPS CUT IN 1-INCH PIECES. LINQUICA OR ANDOUILLE SAUSAGE, DICED AND SAUTÉED WITH SLICED GREEN ONIONS, CAN BE ADDED TO THIS DISH ALONG WITH SEAFOOD.

THE MAC 'N CHEESE RECIPE WITHOUT THE SEAFOOD AND SAUSAGE APPEALS TO ALL PALATES AND AGES.

To make the sauce, melt butter in a large saucepan. Add flour and whisk on low heat for 2 minutes. Slowly add milk to pan whisking until the sauce is thickened and smooth. Bring to a boil and reduce heat. Simmer sauce, whisking occasionally, for 20 minutes. Add cheeses, salt and pepper; stir until cheese is melted.

Preheat oven to 375°. In a skillet, melt butter and sauté shallots and garlic until softened. Add lobster and sauté quickly to heat.

Add cooked pasta to the cheese sauce; mix to coat pasta with sauce. Add shallots and lobster; combine well. Spoon into an ovenproof casserole.

Mix together breadcrumbs and Parmesan cheese; sprinkle mixture over the cavatelli and cheese. Bake until sauce is bubbling and the top is golden brown, 30 to 35 minutes.

pasta fagioli

2 tablespoons olive oil

½ cup diced onion

2 to 3 garlic cloves, minced

1 pound Italian sausage, casings removed and cut into chunks

6 cups chicken stock

1 (14.5-ounce) can diced Italian tomatoes, undrained

1 (15.5-ounce) can cannellini or great Northern beans, drained and
    rinsed

Kosher salt and freshly ground black pepper to taste

3 tablespoons chopped fresh basil

1 cup ditalini pasta

Extra virgin olive oil

Grated Parmesan cheese

GARNISH: Chopped fresh basil

VARATION:

A MIXTURE OF ITALIAN, CHORIZO AND ANDOUILLE SAUSAGE CAN BE SUBSTITUTED IN THIS RECIPE.

In a large saucepan, heat oil and sauté onion until softened. Add garlic and sauté 1 minute. Remove to a bowl with slotted spoon. In same skillet, sauté sausage and drain off fat. Add chicken stock, tomatoes and reserved onion mixture; simmer 30 minutes. Add beans, salt, pepper and basil.

In a large pot of salted boiling water, cook pasta al dente; drain. Spoon pasta into warmed bowls, ladle sausage and bean mixture over pasta. Drizzle with a generous amount of extra virgin olive oil. Top with Parmesan cheese and fresh basil.

kid-friendly

cranberry rice

1 to 2 tablespoons canola oil

2 garlic cloves, minced

1 cup chopped onion

2 cups long-grain white rice

3 cups chicken stock

Kosher salt and freshly ground black pepper to taste

½ cup dried cranberries

½ cup chopped green onions

½ cup pine nuts, toasted

Add oil to a 2-quart saucepan; sauté garlic and onions until onions are translucent. Add the rice, stock, salt and pepper; cover and bring to a boil. Reduce heat to simmer and cook, covered, for 20 minutes. Remove from heat but keep covered for an additional 20 minutes. Toss the rice with the cranberries and green onions. Stir in pine nuts.

chili and cheese rice

1 cup chopped onion

4 tablespoons butter

4 cups freshly cooked long-grain white rice

2 cups sour cream

1 cup cottage cheese

1 large bay leaf, crumbled

Kosher salt and freshly ground black pepper to taste

3 (4-ounce) cans green chiles, drained and sliced in half lengthwise, leaving seeds

2 cups grated sharp Cheddar cheese

GARNISH: Chopped parsley

Preheat oven to 375°. Lightly oil a 9 x 13 x 2-inch baking dish. Sauté onion in butter until golden. Remove from heat and stir in hot rice, sour cream, cottage cheese, bay leaf, salt and pepper. Toss lightly to mix. Layer ½ of rice mixture in the baking dish, then ½ of chiles. Sprinkle with ½ of cheese. Repeat layers. Bake uncovered for 25 minutes or until hot and bubbly. Sprinkle with chopped parsley.

asian rice salad

¼ **cup soy sauce**

1½ **teaspoons Worcestershire sauce**

1 **tablespoon sugar**

1 **teaspoon canola oil**

½ **teaspoon kosher salt**

½ **pound fresh snow peas**

1½ **cups long-grain rice, cooked in chicken stock**

1 **cup cherry tomatoes, halved (optional)**

¾ **cup diced red onion**

1 **yellow bell pepper, diced**

1 **cup sliced fresh mushrooms**

1 **(5-ounce) can water chestnuts, drained and sliced**

¼ **cup minced fresh parsley**

In a bowl, whisk together soy sauce, Worcestershire sauce, sugar, oil and salt; set aside.

In a pan of simmering water, blanch snow peas for 1 minute. Drain and immediately cover with ice water; drain again. Cut snow peas into bite-size pieces.

Combine snow peas, rice, tomatoes, red onion, bell pepper, mushrooms, water chestnuts and parsley with soy mixture. Toss well. The salad can be chilled or served immediately.

lemon rice pilaf

2½ tablespoons olive oil

¾ cup minced onion

1½ cups long-grain white or brown rice

2½ cups chicken stock

¼ cup fresh lemon juice

1¾ teaspoons grated lemon zest

¼ teaspoon kosher salt

½ teaspoon freshly ground black pepper

¼ cup chopped fresh parsley

¼ cup slivered or sliced almonds, lightly toasted

Extra virgin olive oil

GARNISH: Parmesan curls

In a saucepan, heat olive oil. Add onions and sauté on medium heat until tender and translucent, about 10 minutes. Add rice and sauté 2 minutes to coat with oil. Add stock, lemon juice, zest, salt and pepper. Cover pan and simmer on low, about 20 minutes, until liquid is absorbed.

Remove from heat. Add parsley, fluff rice and let stand 5 minutes. Add almonds, drizzle with oil and toss. Serve with Parmesan curls for garnish.

red rice with bacon

1 tablespoon olive oil

1 large onion, finely chopped

½ (0.7-ounce) package of dry Italian salad dressing mix

30 ounces tomato or tomato-vegetable juice

1 cup long-grain white rice

4 tablespoons butter

½ cup grated Parmesan cheese

10 slices bacon, cooked until crisp, crumbled

Preheat oven to 375°. Heat oil in a pan and sauté onions until translucent. Add dressing mix and juice; cook on medium-low heat, stirring, for about 4 minutes. Add rice and butter; continue cooking until butter has melted.

Pour mixture into a 2½-quart oiled casserole dish and top with Parmesan cheese. Bake for 30 minutes; top with bacon and bake an additional 5 minutes.

"What do you do in Boca Grande all day?"—is a question a working

New Yorker might ask a retiree in Boca Grande, assuming the answer would be:

read the paper, play golf, and go to cocktail parties. The more accurate answer would

likely include a variety of cultural, intellectual, and community activities—

The Boca Grande Woman's Club, Lifelong Learning, the Literature Forum,

the Royal Palm Players, the Art Alliance, writer's groups, book clubs, study groups,

physical therapy, Pilates, cooking classes, political lectures, trips to

Sarasota to theater and opera, various board meetings—and sometimes,

read the paper, play golf, and go to cocktail parties.

wild rice in paradise

1 cup golden raisins

½ cup dry sherry

4⅔ cups chicken stock, divided

1 cup wild rice

6 tablespoons butter, divided

1 cup brown rice

1 cup slivered almonds

½ cup chopped fresh parsley

Kosher salt and freshly ground black pepper to taste

NOTE:

GOLDEN RAISINS, DRY SHERRY
AND CRUNCHY ALMONDS
COMPLEMENT THE EARTHY
FLAVOR OF THE RICE. THIS IS A
PERFECT ACCOMPANIMENT TO
POULTRY OR GAME.

Heat raisins and sherry in a small saucepan to boiling. Reduce heat and simmer for 5 minutes. Set aside.

Bring 2 cups chicken stock to a boil. Place wild rice, boiling stock and 2 tablespoons butter in the top of a double boiler set over simmering water. Cook covered for 1 hour. Bring remaining 2⅔ cups chicken stock to a boil. Add brown rice and 2 tablespoons butter. Heat to boiling. Reduce heat to low and cook, covered, until all stock is absorbed, about 50 minutes.

Sauté almonds in remaining 2 tablespoons butter in a small skillet over low heat until lightly toasted. Combine wild rice, brown rice, raisins with sherry, almonds and parsley in a large bowl. Season to taste with salt and pepper and serve immediately.

mediterranean couscous

Dressing

1 garlic clove, chopped

½ teaspoon kosher salt

1 cup stemmed fresh parsley, packed

½ cup fresh lemon juice

¼ cup red wine vinegar

1 teaspoon curry powder

1 teaspoon sugar

¾ teaspoon ground cinnamon

½ teaspoon cumin

½ teaspoon freshly ground black pepper

1 cup extra virgin olive oil

NOTE:

ISRAELI COUSCOUS IS
VERSATILE MEDITERRANEAN
PASTA UNIQUELY TOASTED IN
AN OPEN FLAME OVEN THAT
ALLOWS IT TO ABSORB LIQUIDS
WHILE REMAINING AL DENTE.

Couscous

1 small onion, chopped

2 tablespoons olive oil

1 (8.8-ounce) package Israeli couscous

2 cups vegetable or chicken stock

⅔ cup dried currants

⅔ cup pine nuts, toasted

1 cup kalamata olives, sliced

To make the dressing, mash the garlic and salt to a paste. Place
in the bowl of a food processor; add parsley and mince. Blend in
lemon juice, vinegar, curry, sugar, cinnamon, cumin and pepper.
With processor running, add oil through the feed tube in a steady
stream.

For the couscous, sauté onion in 2 tablespoons olive oil until
softened. Add couscous and stir until brown. Bring stock to a boil
and add to couscous, cover and simmer 8 to 10 minutes. Add
currants, olives and pine nuts to the warm mixture. Toss to combine.
Add dressing to taste and toss again. Cover and refrigerate until
chilled. Remove from the refrigerator 1 hour before serving.

couscous for cruising

3½ cups couscous

4½ cups boiling water

1 tablespoon olive oil

1 cup slivered blanched almonds, toasted

1 cup dried apricots, thinly sliced

1 cup golden raisins

¼ cup orange zest (about 1 orange)

¼ cup roughly chopped mint

1 teaspoon ground cumin or to taste

6 tablespoons fresh lemon juice

6 tablespoons extra virgin olive oil

Kosher salt and freshly ground black pepper to taste

Place couscous in a large bowl. Pour boiling water over couscous. Cover tightly and allow to soak for 15 minutes or until water is absorbed. Fluff couscous with a fork. Rub hands with 1 tablespoon of olive oil. Gently rub couscous between fingers to break up lumps. Add almonds, apricots, raisins, orange zest, mint, cumin, lemon juice, olive oil, salt and pepper. Mix gently until combined. Serve at room temperature.

keen on quinoa

Serves 8

2 cups chicken or vegetable stock

1 cup quinoa, rinsed

2 tablespoons olive oil

¼ cup chopped onion

1 medium zucchini, diced

½ pint grape tomatoes, halved

1 (15-ounce) can white beans, drained and rinsed

2 cups arugula or baby spinach

¼ cup heavy cream

Kosher salt and freshly ground black pepper to taste

¾ cup grated Parmesan cheese, divided

⅓ cup roughly chopped parsley

NOTE:

QUINOA (KEEN-WAH) WAS
A STAPLE IN THE DIET OF THE
ANCIENT INCAS. HAILED AS
A "SUPER GRAIN", QUINOA
CONTAINS MORE PROTEIN
THAN ANY OTHER GRAIN. IT
CAN BE FOUND IN NATURAL
FOOD STORES.

Bring stock and quinoa to a boil. Cover, lower heat and simmer 15 to 20 minutes until stock is absorbed. Set aside.

Heat a large skillet over medium heat. Add olive oil and onion; cook for 5 minutes. Add zucchini and tomatoes. Cook another 5 minutes, until tomatoes are soft. Add beans, arugula, cream, salt and pepper. Cook and stir until beans are warmed through. Add quinoa and ½ cup Parmesan cheese. Toss to combine.

Serve topped with parsley and remaining Parmesan cheese.

vegetables

asparagus with toasted pine nuts

1 pound fresh asparagus

3 tablespoons pine nuts

¼ cup olive oil

1 tablespoon fresh lemon juice

1 garlic clove, crushed

½ teaspoon dried oregano

½ teaspoon dried basil

½ teaspoon kosher salt

Freshly ground black pepper to taste

Rinse asparagus well under cold running water and snap off tough ends. Steam, covered, 5 minutes until crisp-tender. Toast pine nuts in a heavy skillet over medium heat for 3 minutes until golden brown, tossing frequently. Set aside.

Whisk olive oil, lemon juice, garlic, oregano, basil, salt and pepper in a small saucepan. Cook over medium heat 3 minutes or until hot; do not boil. Toss drained asparagus with the warm vinaigrette and place on a serving dish. Let stand at room temperature until serving time. Can be made early in the day and basted occasionally. Sprinkle with pine nuts.

broccoli rabe with black olives and lemon zest

2 (1-pound) bunches broccoli rabe, thick stems discarded

2 tablespoons olive oil, plus more for drizzling

6 garlic cloves, minced

½ teaspoon red pepper flakes

½ cup pitted oil-cured black olives, chopped

1 teaspoon finely grated lemon zest

Kosher salt to taste

2 tablespoons grated Parmesan cheese

NOTE:

BROCCOLI RABE (*RAHB*) IS RELATED TO BOTH THE CABBAGE AND TURNIP FAMILY. THE LEAFY GREEN VEGETABLE HAS SCATTERED CLUSTERS OF TINY BROCCOLI-LIKE BUDS.

Cook the broccoli rabe in a large pot of boiling water until it is bright green, about 1 minute. Drain the rabe, reserving ½ cup of the cooking water.

In a large skillet, heat the 2 tablespoons of oil. Add the garlic and red pepper flakes and cook over moderately low heat until fragrant, about 1 minute. Add broccoli rabe and the reserved cooking water, cover and simmer over moderately low heat until tender, about 10 minutes. Stir in the olives and lemon zest and season with salt. Transfer to a serving dish and drizzle with oil. Sprinkle with the Parmesan cheese and serve.

broccoli with raisin vinaigrette

Serves 4 to 6

4 tablespoons extra virgin olive oil

2 tablespoons sherry wine vinegar

½ cup raisins

1 tablespoon water

½ teaspoon ground cumin

Kosher salt and freshly ground black pepper to taste

2 bunches broccoli, cut into flowerets

In a blender, combine olive oil, vinegar, raisins, water, cumin, salt and pepper. Blend until raisins are finely chopped, about 30 seconds. Season with salt and pepper.

Steam broccoli until just tender. Toss with raisin vinaigrette and adjust seasoning. Serve at room temperature.

truffled brussels sprouts

Serves 8

2½ pounds Brussels sprouts, shredded

1 cup butter

Kosher salt and freshly ground black pepper

1 tablespoon fresh lemon juice

1 tablespoon truffle oil or to taste

Shred the Brussels sprouts with the slicing blade of a food processor. In a large skillet, melt butter. Add Brussels sprouts and season with salt and pepper. Sauté over moderate heat until tender. Remove from heat and stir in lemon juice and truffle oil.

NOTE:

TRUFFLE OIL IS A HIGH-QUALITY OLIVE OIL THAT HAS BEEN INFUSED WITH THE FLAVOR OF EITHER WHITE OR BLACK TRUFFLES. IT HAS AN EARTHY FLAVOR AND SHOULD BE USED SPARINGLY. THE WHITE OIL IS LIKELY TO HAVE A BIT OF A PEPPERY TASTE. ITS BEST USE IS SUMMED UP IN ONE WORD-DRIZZLE.

brussels sprout and cauliflower gratin

Vegetables

1½ pounds Brussels sprouts, trimmed and quartered lengthwise through core

1 (1½-pound) head of cauliflower, trimmed and cut into small flowerets

Sauce

2¾ cups heavy cream

½ cup chopped shallots

1 tablespoon chopped fresh sage

Kosher salt and freshly ground black pepper to taste

Breadcrumb Topping

1½ tablespoons olive oil

½ cup plain dry bread crumbs

½ cup pine nuts, lightly toasted

1 tablespoon chopped fresh parsley

3 cups grated Parmesan cheese, divided

To prepare the vegetables, fill a large bowl with ice and cold water. Cook Brussels sprouts in a large pot of boiling water for 3 minutes. Add cauliflower to this pot and cook 3 additional minutes until vegetables are crisp-tender. Drain. Transfer vegetables to a bowl of ice water and allow to cool. Drain well.

For the sauce, combine cream, shallots and sage in a large saucepan and bring to a boil. Reduce heat; simmer until mixture is reduced to 2¹/₂ cups, about 10 minutes. Season with salt and pepper. Remove from heat and cool slightly.

To prepare the topping, heat oil in a large nonstick skillet over medium heat. Add breadcrumbs; stir until they begin to brown, about 2 minutes. Transfer to a bowl; cool. Stir in pine nuts and parsley.

Preheat oven to 375°. To assemble, butter a 9 x 13 x 2-inch glass baking dish; arrange half of vegetables in dish. Sprinkle with salt and pepper and half of the Parmesan cheese. Repeat layer with remaining vegetables and cheese. Pour sauce mixture evenly over top. Cover gratin with foil. This dish can be prepared a day in advance to this step. Bring to room temperature before baking.

Bake covered for 40 minutes. Uncover; sprinkle breadcrumb topping over and bake uncovered 15 minutes longer.

cauliflower with kalamata vinaigrette

1 (2½ to 3 pound) head of cauliflower

¼ cup extra virgin olive oil, divided

Kosher salt and freshly ground black pepper to taste

1 garlic clove

1 to 2 tablespoons fresh lemon juice

¼ cup finely chopped pitted Kalamata olives

Preheat oven to 450°. Place rack in lower third of the oven. Cut cauliflower from top to bottom into ³/₄-inch thick slices. Place on a foil-lined 10 x 15 x 1-inch baking sheet and brush with 2 tablespoons oil; sprinkle with salt and pepper. Roast, turning once or twice, until golden and just tender, about 25 minutes.

While cauliflower roasts, mince and mash garlic to a paste with a pinch of salt. Whisk together with lemon juice, remaining oil, olives, salt and pepper to taste. Drizzle vinaigrette over roasted cauliflower.

honey and soy glazed carrots

Serves 8

2 pounds carrots, peeled and cut into sticks, 2-inches x ½-inch

2 tablespoons butter

2 tablespoons soy sauce

1½ tablespoons honey

Kosher salt and freshly ground black pepper to taste

Cook the carrots in boiling water until tender, about 8 minutes; drain. In a large skillet, melt the butter. Stir in the carrots and soy sauce and cook over high heat until the carrots are browned in spots, about 2 minutes. Stir in the honey and cook until the carrots are glazed, about 2 minutes longer. Season to taste.

sunshine carrot custard

¾ **pound carrots, coarsely chopped (about 3 cups)**

3 **tablespoons sugar**

1 **tablespoon butter, room temperature**

1 **teaspoon orange zest**

½ **teaspoon kosher salt**

2 **whole eggs**

2 **egg yolks**

1½ **cups heavy cream**

¼ **cup orange marmalade**

2 **tablespoons butter, cut into tiny bits**

NOTE:

CARROT CUSTARD, GARNISHED WITH PARSLEY, IS A VERY ATTRACTIVE ADDITION TO A BUFFET.

Preheat oven to 350°. Cook the carrots in boiling water until soft enough to be easily puréed. Drain them thoroughly. Purée the carrots, sugar and butter in the bowl of a food processor. Fold in the orange zest and salt.

In another bowl, beat the whole eggs and yolks together and slowly stir in the cream and marmalade. Add the carrot purée, stirring thoroughly. Adjust the seasoning.

Pour carrot mixture into a buttered, shallow 6-cup casserole. Dot with bits of butter. Bake in the center of the oven about 40 minutes until the filling is set. Let cool for at least 20 minutes.

barbecued onions

Makes 4 cups

4 large sweet onions

3 tablespoons butter, divided

½ cup ketchup

2 tablespoons honey

Cook onions in a steamer or boil until tender. Slice the onions thickly and sauté in a skillet with 1 tablespoon of butter until golden. Drain and place in a baking dish.

Preheat oven to 350°. In a small saucepan, mix ketchup, honey and remaining 2 tablespoons butter. Heat and pour over the onions. Bake 30 minutes, basting often.

CHEF TIP:

GRILLED BURGERS, RIBS OR SAUSAGES WILL ALL BE ENHANCED BY THE ADDITION OF THESE BARBECUED ONIONS.

farm stand corn sauté

Serves 6

2 tablespoons olive oil

½ cup chopped red onion

1 small orange bell pepper, diced

1 small green bell pepper, diced

2 tablespoons butter

5 ears fresh corn, kernels removed (about 4 cups)

1½ teaspoons kosher salt

1 teaspoon freshly ground black pepper

2 tablespoons julienned fresh basil

Heat the olive oil over medium heat in a large sauté pan. Add the onion and sauté for 5 minutes, until the onion is soft. Stir in the orange and green peppers and sauté for 2 more minutes. Add the butter to the pan and allow it to melt. Over medium heat, add the corn, salt and pepper; cook, stirring occasionally, for 5 to 7 minutes. Adjust seasoning. Gently stir in the basil. Serve hot.

corn and tomato tart

Pie Crust

¾ cup flour

6 tablespoons butter

¼ teaspoon kosher salt

2 tablespoons cold water

Tart Filling

½ cup chopped onion

1 garlic clove, chopped

3 tablespoons olive oil

5 ears of corn, kernels cut off

Kosher salt and freshly ground black pepper to taste

¼ cup grated Cheddar cheese

½ pint cherry tomatoes, cut in half

3 green onions, chopped

2 eggs

½ cup milk

½ cup heavy cream

Preheat oven to 375°. In the bowl of a food processor, pulse together flour, butter and salt until mixture resembles coarse meal. Add water and pulse until the mixture forms a ball. Roll out dough and place in a 10-inch pie plate. Cover with parchment paper and a handful of dried beans or pie weights. Bake 15 minutes. Let crust cool and remove weights.

For the filling, in a medium saucepan over medium heat, sauté onion and garlic in olive oil until onion is translucent, 3 to 5 minutes. Add corn kernels and cook about 8 minutes. Season to taste with salt and pepper. Put half of the corn mixture into the baked pie crust. Layer grated cheese evenly on top. Add remaining corn mixture. Scatter cherry tomatoes and green onions on top. In a small bowl, whisk together eggs, milk and cream; pour over tart. Bake 30 minutes at 375°until tart is golden brown.

eggplant and lentils with pomegranate molasses

Serves 6

Pomegranate Molasses

4 cups pomegranate juice

½ cup sugar

¼ cup lemon juice

NOTE:

THIS DISH WORKS WELL AS A
VEGETARIAN ENTRÉE.

Eggplant and Lentils

½ cup lentils

⅔ cup olive oil

1 (1½-pound) eggplant, skin on or peeled if preferred, cut into 1-inch cubes

1 onion, finely chopped

4 garlic cloves, minced

2 tomatoes, chopped

2 long green chiles such as Anaheims, stemmed, seeded and coarsely chopped

1 tablespoon tomato paste

¼ teaspoon red pepper flakes

Kosher salt and freshly ground black pepper to taste

Chicken stock

¼ cup pomegranate molasses or to taste

2 tablespoons chopped mint leaves

For the pomegranate molasses, in a large uncovered sauce pan, heat pomegranate juice, sugar and lemon juice on medium-high until the sugar has dissolved and the juice simmers. Reduce heat enough to maintain a simmer. Simmer for about 1 hour, or until the juice has a syrup consistency and has reduced to about 1 cup. Pour into a jar and let cool. Store in refrigerator or at room temperature.

In a small saucepan, cover the lentils with 2-inches of water and bring to a boil. Do not add salt or the lentils will not soften when they cook. Reduce the heat to medium-low and simmer until tender, about 15 minutes. Drain the lentils.

228 hearts of palm

Heat a sauté pan over medium-high heat. Add 2 or 3 tablespoons of olive oil and cook eggplant in batches, browning on all sides. Add more olive oil as needed. Remove the eggplant from the pan and lower the heat to medium-low.

Add the onion to the pan and sauté until soft, about 5 minutes. Add the eggplant and lentils; add garlic, tomatoes, chiles, tomato paste, red pepper flakes, salt and pepper to taste. Cook for another 6 to 8 minutes. If mixture seems too dry, chicken stock can be added to moisten. Remove from heat. Add pomegranate molasses and mint. Can be served hot, warm or at room temperature.

warm potatoes with olives and lemon

Serves 4

1½ pounds Yukon gold or red potatoes

Kosher salt to taste

2 tablespoons dry vermouth

½ cup kalamata olives, pitted

1 cup grape tomatoes, halved

4 green onions, including greens, chopped

Grated zest of 1 lemon

Freshly ground black pepper to taste

2 tablespoons extra virgin olive oil

Coarse sea salt

Cook scrubbed, whole, unpeeled potatoes in salted water until tender, about 20 minutes. Drain on a rack and allow potatoes to cool enough to handle. They must stay warm, so work quickly. Peel the potatoes and cut into thick slices, about ½-inch. As you finish each one, place it in a mixing bowl and sprinkle with dry vermouth. Add the olives, tomatoes, green onions and grated lemon zest. Season with pepper and drizzle with olive oil. Transfer to a serving platter and sprinkle with sea salt.

park avenue potatoes

6 medium potatoes, unpeeled, boiled, drained and refrigerated
    24 hours

4 tablespoons butter

2 cups shredded Cheddar cheese

2 cups sour cream

½ teaspoon kosher salt

⅛ teaspoon freshly ground black pepper

½ onion, minced

NOTE:

THIS RECIPE BEGINS WITH
COOKED POTATOES, WHICH
HAVE BEEN REFRIGERATED FOR
24 HOURS. DON'T MISS THIS
IMPORTANT FIRST STEP.

Preheat oven to 350°. Melt the butter in a heavy saucepan or double boiler. Add cheese, sour cream, salt, pepper and onion. Stir over low heat until blended. Peel and grate the potatoes on a coarse grater. Stir into the cheese mixture. Oil a 1 to 1½-quart baking dish. Pour in the potato mixture. Bake 45 minutes.

Shopping has been described as the female equivalent of hunting. The endless hours spent searching, the excitement of discovery, the bagging of the perfect trophy—at the right price. Boca Bargains, one of the supporting financial engines of The Boca Grande Woman's Club, is a treasure trove for shoppers. People come from far and wide to pour through the nearly-new castaways from the closets of Boca Grande. A carved wooden headboard, a Kenneth Jay Lane pin, St. John knits, Chanel suits, Hermes ties, Gucci scarves, estate linens, children's winter coats, doggie beds and all manner of decorative arts. Begun as a garage sale in 1975 with a profit of $375, Boca Bargains annually takes in more than $100,000. These proceeds help to support the Club's charitable giving to the community.

fingerling potatoes and asparagus

¼ cup buttermilk

2 tablespoons fresh lemon juice

1 teaspoon sugar

1 teaspoon Dijon mustard

¾ teaspoon kosher salt

1¼ teaspoons freshly ground black pepper

½ cup extra virgin olive oil

2 tablespoons finely chopped green onion

1 tablespoon fresh tarragon

2 pounds fingerling potatoes, unpeeled

1 tablespoon olive oil

1 pound asparagus, stalks trimmed, cut into thirds

Kosher salt and freshly ground black pepper to taste

In a small bowl, mix buttermilk, lemon juice, sugar, mustard, salt and pepper until well combined. In a slow, steady stream, whisk in oil. Add green onion and tarragon. Chill up to 2 days. Let stand for 30 minutes at room temperature before using.

Gently cook the potatoes for about 10 minutes; do not over-cook. Remove from the heat and drain. When the potatoes are cool enough to handle, slice them in half diagonally.

While the potatoes are cooking, heat the oil in a sauté pan over medium-high heat. Add the asparagus, stir and sauté for about 4 minutes. Remove from the heat and add to the warm potatoes; toss gently and season with salt and pepper. Add desired amount of dressing. Toss and serve warm or at room temperature.

weezy's cheesy potatoes

1½ pounds frozen cubed hash brown potatoes, thawed

1 cup half & half or milk

½ cup butter

½ pound American or processed cheese loaf, cubed

4 ounces sharp Cheddar cheese, grated

1 to 2 (4-ounce) cans chopped green chilies (optional)

CHEF TIP:

THE BAKED POTATO CASSEROLE "HOLDS" WELL IN THE OVEN AT 175°.

Arrange potatoes in an oiled 9 x 13 x 2-inch baking dish. Combine milk, butter and cheeses in a saucepan. Heat on medium-low until cheese is melted. Add chilies, if desired, and pour over the potatoes. Mix gently to combine. Cover and refrigerate for at least 1 hour.

Preheat oven to 350°. Bake uncovered for 1 to 1¼ hours.

roasted spiced sweet potatoes

1 teaspoon coriander seeds

½ teaspoon fennel seeds

½ teaspoon dried oregano

½ teaspoon red pepper flakes

1 teaspoon kosher salt

2 pounds medium sweet potatoes, peeled

3 tablespoons canola oil

Preheat oven to 425°. Coarsely grind coriander, fennel, oregano and red pepper flakes in an electric spice grinder or with a mortar and pestle; add salt.

Cut potatoes lengthwise into 1-inch wedges. Toss wedges with oil and spices in a large roasting pan and roast in the middle of the oven for 20 minutes. Turn wedges over with a spatula and roast until tender and slightly golden, 15 to 20 minutes.

gingered sweet potatoes

Serves 4 to 6

3 tablespoons butter

¼ cup heavy cream

3 tablespoons finely chopped fresh ginger

3 tablespoons finely chopped garlic

2 pounds (about 3 large) sweet potatoes

Kosher salt and freshly ground black pepper to taste

In a small saucepan over low heat, melt butter and add heavy cream. Remove from heat and add ginger and garlic. Set aside to blend flavors.

In water to cover, boil sweet potatoes, whole and unpeeled, until tender in the center when pierced with a knife, about 30 minutes. Cool potatoes until they can be handled. Peel and place in medium saucepan, covered to keep warm.

Place a fine-meshed strainer over a medium bowl. Pour ginger and garlic mixture into strainer and press on the solids to extract as much liquid as possible. Discard solids and add liquid to the sweet potatoes. Place the saucepan of potatoes over low heat. Mash them until they are smooth; reheat. Season with salt and pepper. Serve hot.

tomatoes with "aïoli"

Serves 4

⅓ cup mayonnaise

1 to 2 garlic cloves, finely minced

¾ teaspoon fresh lemon Juice

2 tomatoes (about 1½ pounds), cut in half, crosswise

1½ tablespoons olive oil

Kosher salt and freshly ground black pepper to taste

CHEF TIP:
THE TOMATOES CAN BE
GRILLED INSTEAD OF BROILED.
THE LUSCIOUS "AÏOLI" MAKES
THIS A SPECTACULAR DISH.

Whisk mayonnaise, garlic and lemon juice in a small bowl to blend. Brush cut sides of tomatoes with oil and place on a broiler pan, cut sides down. Broil tomatoes until hot, juicy and tender, turning them, about 3 minutes per side. Transfer to a plate and season with salt and pepper. Top each tomato half with a dollop of garlic mayonnaise.

scalloped tomatoes

5 tablespoons olive oil, divided

2 cups cubed French bread, crusts trimmed if desired

1 (14.5-ounce) can diced tomatoes, undrained

2 garlic cloves, minced

2 tablespoons sugar

Kosher salt and freshly ground black pepper to taste

½ cup julienned fresh basil leaves

1 cup grated Parmesan cheese

Preheat oven to 350°. Heat 3 tablespoons olive oil in a large skillet over medium heat. Add the bread cubes and stir to coat evenly with the oil. Sauté until lightly browned all over, 5 to 7 minutes. Add the tomatoes, garlic and sugar. Cook, stirring frequently for 5 minutes. Season with salt and pepper; stir in the basil and remove from the heat.

Transfer the tomato mixture to a buttered, shallow 1½-quart casserole. Sprinkle the Parmesan cheese over the top and drizzle 2 tablespoons olive oil on cheese. Bake until bubbling and lightly browned, 35 to 40 minutes. Serve hot.

tomato parmesan gratin

4 tomatoes, sliced ¼-inch thick

Kosher salt and freshly ground black pepper to taste

8 slices of bacon, cooked crisp, drained and crumbled

3 tablespoons julienned fresh basil or 1 tablespoon dried

¾ cup grated Parmesan cheese

¾ cup mayonnaise

⅓ cup crushed round buttery crackers

Preheat oven to 350°. Sprinkle tomatoes with salt and drain well on paper towels. Generously oil a pie plate with olive oil. Arrange half of the tomatoes in a single layer. Lightly season with salt and pepper. Sprinkle with half the bacon and basil; continue layering. Combine Parmesan cheese and mayonnaise. Spread over top layer of tomatoes. Sprinkle crushed crackers over the top and bake until crumbs begin to brown, about 30 minutes.

breton tomatoes

4 large plum tomatoes

3 tablespoons butter

1 tablespoon chopped fresh parsley

1 tablespoon chopped fresh basil

½ teaspoon sugar

½ teaspoon kosher salt

½ teaspoon freshly ground black pepper

NOTE:

THIS DISH GIVES WINTER TOMATOES A REAL FLAVOR BOOST.

Cut tomatoes in half crosswise. Slice a thin piece from either end so tomato halves can stand up. In a skillet, sauté tomatoes in butter on both cut sides.

Combine parsley, basil, sugar, salt and pepper and sprinkle over wider ends of tomatoes. Cook 2 minutes longer, with wider ends up. Serve.

zucchini alla pancetta

8 zucchini (about 6-inches in length), cut into ½-inch slices

2 tablespoons kosher salt

¼ cup olive oil

1 tablespoon butter

8 ounces thinly sliced pancetta, coarsely chopped

1 medium red onion, thinly sliced

¼ cup chopped fresh parsley

1 large garlic clove, finely chopped

1 (16-ounce) can whole tomatoes, drained

Kosher salt and freshly ground black pepper to taste

Place zucchini slices on a baking sheet and sprinkle with salt. Let rest for 1 hour. Rinse the zucchini in a colander and pat dry with paper towels.

Heat the oil and butter; add pancetta and sauté for 10 minutes. Add the onion and sauté 2 to 3 minutes. Add the parsley and garlic and cook for 5 minutes, stirring frequently. Add the tomatoes and crush each one with a spoon. Put a layer of zucchini on top, cover and cook another 5 minutes. Uncover and mix the ingredients well; simmer 15 minutes. Season with salt and pepper. Serve immediately.

desserts

captain's cashew tart

Crust

1⅔ cups all-purpose flour

¼ cup sugar

½ teaspoon kosher salt

10 tablespoons butter, chilled and cubed

2 egg yolks

2 teaspoons ice water

Filling

½ cup sugar

2 tablespoons water

2 tablespoons light corn syrup

2 tablespoons butter

¼ cup heavy cream

1 cup roasted, salted cashews

GARNISH: Coarse sea salt

Chocolate shavings

To prepare crust, combine flour, sugar and salt in the bowl of a food processor. Add butter and pulse until the mixture resembles coarse meal. Combine egg yolks and water. With motor running, gradually add egg and water mixture to the flour until it gathers into a ball. Remove dough, press into a disk and cover in plastic wrap. Refrigerate 1 hour.

Preheat oven to 375°. On a well floured surface, roll dough into a 10 to 12-inch circle. Place dough in a 9-inch tart pan with removable bottom. Press dough against sides of pan. Trim away and discard excess dough. Chill shell until firm, 5 minutes. Bake pastry shell 15 minutes; cool.

For the filling, place sugar, water and corn syrup in a small pan over medium heat. Swirl pan lightly to mix. Simmer mixture until it turns the color of tea, about 5 minutes. Remove caramel from heat; stir in the butter. Add cream; stir until caramel is smooth. Add cashews and pour caramel filling evenly into baked shell. Allow tart to cool completely. Garnish with sea salt and chocolate shavings.

peaches'n cream pie

Crust

1¼ cups all-purpose flour

½ teaspoon kosher salt

½ cup cold butter, cut into 8 pieces

2 tablespoons sour cream

Filling

3 egg yolks

1 cup sugar

2 tablespoons all-purpose flour

⅓ cup sour cream

4 peaches, peeled and sliced

Preheat oven to 425°. For the crust, combine flour, salt, butter and sour cream in the bowl of a food processor. Process until mixture forms a ball. Pat mixture into a buttered 9-inch pie plate. Prick crust with a fork. Bake 10 minutes and remove from oven.

To prepare the filling, combine egg yolks, sugar, flour and sour cream; mix well. Place peaches in crust and pour sour cream mixture over top. Cover with foil and return to oven. Immediately reduce temperature to 350°. Bake for 40 minutes. Remove foil and continue to bake for another 15 to 20 minutes or until filling is set.

lemon tart with blueberries

Almond Crust

5 ounces almonds, finely chopped

½ cup butter, room temperature

2 tablespoons sugar

1½ cups all-purpose flour

¼ teaspoon kosher salt

1 egg

½ teaspoon almond extract

VARIATION:

BLACKBERRIES, PEACHES OR
OTHER FAVORITE FRUIT CAN BE
SUBSTITUTED FOR BLUEBERRIES
IN THIS TART.

Filling

2 pints blueberries, washed and drained

Sugar to taste

2 cups lemon curd, best quality commercial brand

¾ cup red currant jelly, melted

For the crust, blend almonds, butter, sugar, flour and salt in the bowl of a food processor until well combined. Add egg and almond extract and pulse until well mixed. Press mixture into a buttered 11-inch tart pan with removable bottom. Chill at least 30 minutes.

Preheat oven to 350°. Bake crust until golden brown, 30 minutes. Allow to cool. Combine berries with sugar and set aside.

To assemble the tart, spread lemon curd over crust. Arrange blueberries over lemon curd; lightly brush melted currant jelly over berries.

rhubarb pie

3 eggs, beaten

1½ cups sugar

3 tablespoons all-purpose flour

4 cups rhubarb, cut into very small pieces

1 (9-inch) pie crust, unbaked

Preheat oven to 400°. Mix together egg, sugar and flour. Add rhubarb and combine well. Pour into unbaked pie crust and bake for 30 minutes. Reduce temperature to 325° and check in 20 minutes. Pie is done when filling is just set.

One of the on-going amenities in Boca Grande is the free movie on the big screen

at the Boca Grande Community Center on Tuesday and Thursday nights

and Saturday afternoons. Once, during a particular movie, starring Judi Dench,

about an all-female band playing in London during the Blitz, the women

on the screen sang "Don't Sit Under the Apple Tree With Anyone Else But Me".

Many in the audience that night were World War II veterans and their wives who burst

into song right along with the actors.

chocolate tart

Crust

¾ cup butter

½ cup powdered sugar

2 egg yolks

2 scant cups all-purpose flour

Filling

7 ounces best quality dark bittersweet chocolate, coarsely chopped

10 tablespoons butter

2 whole eggs

3 egg yolks

2 tablespoons sugar

GARNISH: Chocolate curls or grated chocolate

Preheat oven to 350°. For the crust, in the bowl of a food processor, combine butter, sugar and egg yolks. Add flour and process until mixture forms a ball. Form into a disk and wrap in plastic. Chill at least 1½ hours.

Roll pastry and fit into a 9-inch tart pan with a removable bottom. If pastry breaks, pat in place with hands. Bake 25 minutes or until lightly brown.

To prepare the filling, increase oven temperature to 375°. In a saucepan, melt together chocolate and butter. Beat eggs, yolks and sugar vigorously with mixer until thick and fluffy. Add warm chocolate mixture; beat briefly. Pour into pastry shell and return to oven for 5 minutes. Cool to room temperature. Refrigerate until 1 hour before serving.

Garnish with chocolate curls or grated chocolate.

VARIATION:

THE TART CAN BE SERVED TOPPED WITH WHIPPED CREAM, CRÈME FRAÎCHE OR MIXED BERRIES.

NOTE:

CRÈME FRAÎCHE IS AVAILABLE IN THE DAIRY SECTION OF MANY GROCERY STORES OR YOU CAN MAKE YOUR OWN. TO MAKE 1 PINT, IN A GLASS JAR, MIX 2 CUPS HEAVY CREAM AND 4 TABLESPOONS BUTTERMILK. COVER AND ALLOW MIXTURE TO STAND AT ROOM TEMPERATURE FOR 12 HOURS OR UNTIL VERY THICK, THE CONSISTENCY OF SOUR CREAM. REFRIGERATE FOR 36 HOURS BEFORE USING. CRÈME FRAÎCHE IS A DELICIOUS ALTERNATIVE TO WHIPPED CREAM ON DESSERTS.

apple and almond torte

Crust

½ cup butter, room temperature

⅓ cup sugar

¼ teaspoon pure vanilla extract

1 cup all-purpose flour

Filling

1 (8-ounce) package cream cheese, room temperature

½ teaspoon pure vanilla extract

¼ cup sugar

1 egg

Topping

4 cups peeled and sliced Granny Smith apples (about 4 apples)

⅓ cup sugar

½ teaspoon cinnamon

¼ cup slivered almonds

Preheat oven to 350°. To prepare the crust, cream butter with sugar. Mix in vanilla and flour. Press dough into the bottom and 1-inch up the sides of a 9-inch springform pan. (Line bottom of pan with parchment paper if bottom will eventually be removed.)

For the filling, mix cream cheese, vanilla, sugar and egg. The mixture will resemble pudding. Pour filling over crust.

To prepare the topping, mix apple slices with sugar and cinnamon. Arrange slices over filling. Sprinkle with almonds and bake for 10 minutes. Reduce temperature to 300° and bake for 45 minutes longer. Cool before removing side of pan.

pear and walnut galette

Crust

1¼ cups all-purpose flour

2 tablespoons sugar

¼ teaspoon kosher salt

7 tablespoons butter, very cold, diced

3 to 4 tablespoons ice water

Filling

6 tablespoons butter

¾ cup packed brown sugar

1 tablespoon pure vanilla extract

1 teaspoon cinnamon

6 medium Bartlett pears, peeled, halved and cored

½ cup walnuts, toasted

To prepare the crust, place the flour, sugar and salt in the bowl of a food processor and pulse to combine. Add diced butter and process to cut butter into flour (about 10 seconds). Slowly add water through the feed tube just until a ball is formed. Turn dough out onto a floured surface and form into a disk. Wrap with plastic and chill for 2 hours.

Preheat oven to 425°. For the filling, melt butter in an ovenproof 12-inch skillet. Add brown sugar, vanilla and cinnamon. Simmer over medium heat 4 minutes or until mixture thickens.

Cut each pear half into 3 wedges. Arrange pears and nuts in sugar mixture and simmer until slightly soft, about 3 minutes.

On a floured surface, roll pie crust into a 12-inch circle. Place crust over pears and cut several slits in top. Bake the galette for about 35 minutes, until top is golden. Remove from oven and let rest for 5 minutes.

Place a large plate over top of skillet and invert. Serve warm.

cherry berry cobbler

1 cup sugar, divided

2 teaspoons cornstarch

Pinch of kosher salt

1 (10-ounce) package frozen raspberries, thawed and undrained

1 teaspoon fresh lemon juice

1 (16-ounce) can pitted tart cherries, drained

2 cups fresh blueberries

½ cup butter, room temperature

1 cup all-purpose flour

¼ teaspoon kosher salt

Premium vanilla ice cream

Preheat oven to 375°. Combine ½ cup sugar, cornstarch and ⅛ teaspoon salt in a saucepan. Stir in raspberries and lemon juice; bring to a boil. Cook 1 minute, stirring constantly. Stir cherries and blueberries into raspberry mixture and spoon into a buttered 1½-quart baking dish.

Cream butter and ½ cup sugar. Stir in flour and ¼ teaspoon salt, blending just until mixture is like coarse meal. Crumble over berry mixture. Bake for 30 minutes or until top is golden. Serve with vanilla ice cream.

cayo costa key lime cheesecake

Crust

1 cup graham cracker crumbs

3 tablespoons butter, melted

2 tablespoons sugar

NOTE:

EGGS SEPARATE MORE EASILY WHEN THEY ARE COLD. EGG WHITES WILL HAVE GREATER VOLUME IF THEY ARE AT ROOM TEMPERATURE WHEN BEATEN.

Filling

1 envelope unflavored gelatin

¾ cup Key lime juice

1½ cups sugar, divided

4 eggs, room temperature

2 egg yolks, room temperature

2 tablespoons grated Key lime zest

1¼ pounds cream cheese, room temperature

2 egg whites, room temperature

Pinch of kosher salt

GARNISH: Sweetened whipped cream

Twists of Key limes

Preheat oven to 350°. For the crust, combine graham cracker crumbs, melted butter and sugar; mix well. Press crumbs firmly over bottom of a 9-inch springform pan. Bake until lightly golden and fragrant, about 8 minutes. Set aside on a rack to cool.

In a saucepan, combine gelatin and Key lime juice; set aside until the gelatin has softened, about 5 minutes. Heat over medium heat until gelatin is completely dissolved, 1 to 2 minutes. Add 1¼ cups of the sugar, eggs, egg yolks and Key lime zest; whisk thoroughly to combine. Continue cooking over medium heat, whisking frequently, until mixture thickens and is pudding-like, about 4 to 5 minutes. Remove from the heat and transfer to a heatproof bowl.

Using an electric mixer, beat cream cheese until smooth. While mixer is running, add the hot lime mixture, little by little, beating until smooth. Transfer to a clean bowl and cool completely, stirring frequently. Cover with plastic wrap and refrigerate until chilled, stirring every 15 minutes, for about 1 hour.

Using an electric mixer with clean beaters, beat egg whites, salt and remaining ¼ cup of the sugar. Whip on medium-high until stiff peaks form. Remove the lime and cheese mixture from the refrigerator. Fold egg whites into lime mixture gently but thoroughly. Pour mixture over crust. Cover with plastic wrap and refrigerate until set, at least 4 hours or overnight.

Remove from the refrigerator. Run a sharp knife along sides of pan and remove the springform. Spread the whipped cream evenly over the top of the cake. Garnish with mint or Key lime twists.

mocha divine cake

Serves 8

2 cups butter

1 cup plus 2 tablespoons sugar

1 cup plus 2 tablespoons espresso or French roast coffee

12 ounces best quality bittersweet chocolate

4 ounces best quality unsweetened chocolate

8 eggs, slightly beaten

Preheat oven to 350°. Line a 9-inch springform pan with foil. Butter and flour generously. Over low heat melt butter, sugar and coffee. Whisk together thoroughly. Add bittersweet and unsweetened chocolate and continue stirring until melted. Remove from heat. Add eggs and whisk together. Turn into prepared pan. Bake 50 to 55 minutes until top has a crust and is dry to the touch. Serve as soon as cool or refrigerate 12 to 14 hours.

Serve with Raspberry Sauce (see page 260) or fresh raspberries.

cocoa-pistachio layer cake

Cake

½ cup unsweetened cocoa

½ cup boiling water

1¾ cups all-purpose flour

1 teaspoon baking powder

1 teaspoon baking soda

Pinch of kosher salt

½ cup butter, room temperature

2 cups sugar

2 eggs

1 teaspoon pure vanilla extract

1⅓ cups buttermilk

½ cup finely chopped unsalted pistachios or walnuts

Frosting

1 cup heavy cream

⅓ cup light cream

5 tablespoons butter

⅔ cup unsweetened cocoa

2⅔ cups sifted powdered sugar, divided

1 teaspoon light corn syrup

1 teaspoon pure vanilla extract

¼ cup coarsely chopped unsalted pistachios or walnuts

Preheat oven to 350°. For the cake, in a small bowl, mix cocoa with boiling water. Generously butter and flour three 8-inch layer cake pans. Sift together flour, baking powder, baking soda and salt. In a large mixing bowl, combine butter, sugar, eggs and vanilla. Beat on high speed until fluffy. On low speed, add flour mixture in fourths, alternately with buttermilk. Measure 1⅔ cups batter and pour batter into a small bowl; stir in chopped nuts and pour into one of the baking pans. Add cocoa mixture to remaining batter; divide evenly between the other two pans. Bake 30 to 35 minutes. Remove from pans immediately as cake tends to stick to pans; cool.

For the frosting, whip heavy cream until stiff; refrigerate.

Heat light cream until bubbles form; remove from heat. In a bowl, place butter, cocoa, 1½ cups powdered sugar, corn syrup and vanilla. Add the hot light cream and beat until smooth. Add additional sugar until thick enough to spread.

To assemble the cake, place one chocolate layer on cake plate; spread with half of whipped cream. Place nut layer on next; spread with rest of whipped cream. Top with remaining chocolate layer. Spread frosting on sides and top; garnish top edge with coarsely chopped nuts. Refrigerate.

major chocolate cake

Serves 9

7 ounces best quality semisweet chocolate, chopped

4 teaspoons strong coffee

1 cup butter

1 cup sugar

4 eggs

Whipped cream

Preheat oven to 350°. Spray an 8 x 8 x 2-inch glass baking dish with cooking spray and coat lightly with flour. Combine the chocolate, coffee and butter in a microwave-safe bowl. Warm in microwave set on high for 45 seconds or until completely melted. Add sugar and eggs. Whisk vigorously until mixture forms a batter-like consistency. Pour into baking dish and bake for 35 minutes. Serve warm with unsweetened whipped cream.

praline cheesecake

Crust

1¼ cups graham cracker crumbs

¼ cup sugar

¼ cup toasted pecans, chopped

4 tablespoons butter, melted

Filling

3 (8-ounce) packages cream cheese, room temperature

1 cup packed brown sugar

1 (15-ounce) can evaporated milk

2 tablespoons all-purpose flour

1½ teaspoons pure vanilla extract

3 eggs

Topping

1 cup toasted pecan halves

½ cup dark corn syrup

2 tablespoons cornstarch

1 tablespoon brown sugar

½ teaspoon pure vanilla extract

Preheat oven to 350°. For the crust, combine graham cracker crumbs, sugar and pecans. Stir in melted butter. Press over bottom and 1½-inches up sides of a 9-inch springform pan. Bake for 10 minutes.

For the filling, beat together cream cheese, brown sugar, milk, flour and vanilla. Add eggs one at a time; beat until blended and pour into baked crust. Bake 50 to 55 minutes or until set. Cool 30 minutes. Loosen sides and remove rim of pan. Cool completely. Arrange pecan halves on top of cake.

Before serving, combine corn syrup, cornstarch and brown sugar. Cook stirring until thickened and bubbly. Remove from heat. Stir in vanilla and cool slightly.

To serve, spoon some warm sauce over nuts on top of cake. Pass remaining sauce.

gaspar's coconut cake

Cake

3 cups cake flour

1 teaspoon baking powder

¼ teaspoon kosher salt

2½ cups sugar

1½ cups solid vegetable shortening

5 eggs

1 cup milk

2 teaspoons coconut extract

1 cup shredded coconut plus more for sprinkling on the baked cake

Glaze

4 tablespoons butter

1 cup sugar

2 tablespoons light corn syrup

½ cup buttermilk

Butter and flour a tube or Bundt pan, tapping out extra flour. In a large bowl, combine the flour, baking powder and salt; mix well.

In the bowl of an electric mixer, cream sugar and shortening on high speed for 10 minutes, scraping down the sides of the bowl as needed. Turn to low speed and add eggs, one at a time, beating well to combine after each addition. Add the flour mixture in two parts, alternating with the milk, beginning and ending with the flour; beat until combined after each addition. Fold in the coconut extract and 1 cup of coconut. Pour the batter into the prepared pan and place in a cold oven. Set the oven temperature at 300°; bake 1 hour and 25 minutes or until a cake tester comes out clean.

To prepare the glaze, combine butter, sugar, corn syrup and buttermilk in a saucepan. Cook slowly on low heat; do not allow to thicken. Keep warm until the cake is baked.

Remove the cake from the oven; pour the warm glaze over the hot cake. Cover immediately and set aside to cool.

Place a cake plate over the cake pan and quickly invert; remove pan, pouring any remaining glaze over cake. Sprinkle with coconut.

orange timbales

Cake

1 cup butter, room temperature

1½ cups sugar

4 eggs, room temperature

3 cups all-purpose flour

2½ teaspoons baking powder

Pinch of kosher salt

¼ cup milk

Zest of 2 oranges

COMPLIMENTS OF:

EXECUTIVE CHEF

PETER TIMMONS

GASPARILLA INN AND CLUB

BOCA GRANDE, FLORIDA

Sauce

½ cup sugar

½ cup water

2 oranges, zest removed and juiced

½ lemon, juiced

2 teaspoons cornstarch

Premium vanilla ice cream (optional)

Preheat oven to 350°. To prepare the cakes, place butter and sugar in the bowl of a mixer and cream together until white and fluffy. Add eggs, one at a time, beating well to combine.

Sift together the flour, baking powder and salt to ensure the even distribution of the baking powder, and sift again.

Add the flour mixture to the butter and sugar mixture alternately with the milk, beginning and ending with the flour. Beat until well combined. Fold in the orange zest.

Heavily butter 8 to 10 timbale molds or ovenproof glass custard cups and dust them with sugar. Fill the molds approximately half full with cake mixture and place them in a metal baking pan. Carefully add hot water to pan to a depth of about 1-inch. Cover with parchment paper and then foil, being sure to completely seal the pan with the foil. Place the pan on stove top and bring the water just to a boil.

The foil will puff up when water starts to steam. Immediately place pan in oven and bake for 35 to 45 minutes.

For the sauce, place sugar and water in a heavy pot and bring to a boil on the stove top. Cook just until mixture starts to turn a golden color. Remove from heat and add the orange zest, orange juice and lemon juice. Return to heat and bring to a boil; reduce by one-third. Mix cornstarch with 1 to 2 teaspoons of water and add slowly to the sauce, whisking constantly. Simmer until sauce thickens.

To serve, place each cake on a dessert plate; drizzle sauce over and around cake. Add a small scoop of ice cream to each plate, if desired.

warm summer fruit compote with vanilla ice cream

Serves 6 to 8

**8 cups assorted fruit, thickly sliced, skin on
(peaches, plums, apricots, nectarines)**

1 cup blueberries

1 cup raspberries

3 tablespoons sugar

1½ pints premium vanilla ice cream

Preheat oven to 425°. Arrange sliced fruit in a 12-inch gratin baking dish. Top with berries and sprinkle with sugar. Bake until fruit is tender and berry juices are bubbling, 20 to 30 minutes.

Scoop ice cream into dessert bowls and spoon fruit and sauce over top. Fruit can be served warm or at room temperature.

boca lemon pudding cake

Cake

1½ cups buttermilk

1 cup sugar, divided

4 egg yolks

⅓ cup fresh lemon juice

¼ cup all-purpose flour

4 tablespoons butter, melted

⅛ teaspoon kosher salt

3 egg whites

Cream Topping

½ cup whipping cream

1 tablespoon sugar

¼ cup crème fraîche or Greek-style yogurt

GARNISH: Assorted berries

Preheat oven to 350°. To prepare the cake, butter an 8 x 8 x 2-inch glass baking dish. Blend buttermilk, ½ cup sugar, egg yolks, lemon juice, flour, butter and salt in a blender until smooth. Use electric mixer to beat egg whites until soft peaks form. Gradually add remaining ½ cup sugar and beat until stiff but not dry. Gently fold buttermilk mixture into whites in 3 additions (batter will be runny). Pour batter into prepared dish and place dish in roasting pan. Pour enough hot water into roasting pan to come halfway up sides of dish. Bake until top is evenly browned and cake barely moves in center but feels slightly springy to touch, about 45 minutes.

Remove dish from roasting pan. Cool cake completely in baking dish on a rack. Refrigerate until cold, at least 3 hours and up to 6 hours.

For the topping, use an electric mixer to whip together cream and sugar until soft peaks form. Add crème fraîche and continue mixing until just combined. Spoon pudding cake into shallow bowls and add a dollop of cream topping and fresh berries.

sinful chocolate bread pudding

Serves 8

1 loaf bread (1 pound), trimmed of crust and cut into ½-inch cubes
(do not use sourdough bread)

4 eggs

1½ cups milk

2 cups heavy cream

1¼ cups sugar

1 teaspoon pure vanilla extract

1½ cups coarsely chopped best quality bittersweet chocolate

CHEF TIP:

MELT PREMIUM VANILLA ICE
CREAM FOR A QUICK CRÈME
ANGLAISE AND DRIZZLE OVER
THIS PUDDING.

Preheat oven to 375°. Whisk eggs, milk, cream, sugar and vanilla together. Add bread cubes and let soak for about an hour, mixing occasionally, until the bread absorbs the egg mixture. Add the chocolate bits and stir; pour into a 2-quart buttered soufflé dish.

Bake about 1 hour or until pudding is set and golden on top. Pudding is done when knife inserted in center comes out clean.

To serve, spoon pudding onto individual dessert plates.

grilled bananas with
ice cream and bourbon-caramel sauce

Bourbon-Caramel Sauce

1½ cups dark brown sugar, packed

1½ cups heavy whipping cream

3 tablespoons butter

1½ tablespoons honey

1½ vanilla beans, halved lengthwise

1½ tablespoons bourbon

NOTE:

GRILLING THE BANANAS IN
THEIR SKINS MAKES FOR A FUN
PRESENTATION AND MAKES
PREP EASY FOR THE COOK.

Grilled Bananas

5 large bananas, unpeeled

1 quart premium vanilla ice cream

GARNISH: Chopped toasted pecans

To prepare the sauce, combine brown sugar, cream, butter and honey in a heavy large saucepan. Scrape in vanilla seeds; add beans. Stir mixture over medium heat until sugar dissolves. Increase heat and bring to a boil. Reduce heat to medium-low and boil gently until sauce coats a spoon thickly. Reduce to 1³/₄ cups, stirring occasionally, about 25 minutes. Mix in bourbon.

For grilled bananas, prepare grill to medium-high heat. Cut unpeeled bananas in half lengthwise. Arrange, cut side up, on baking sheet. Brush cut sides with caramel sauce. Place bananas, still cut side up, on grill rack. Close grill lid; grill until peels are slightly charred and fruit is tender and beginning to come away from peel, about 4 minutes. (The bananas are equally delicious prepared under a broiler.)

Place 1 banana half, cut-side up, on each plate. Top each with ice cream, warm sauce and pecans.

fruit with limoncello sauce

7 ounces Greek-style yogurt

⅓ cup best commercial brand lemon curd

1 tablespoon honey

½ teaspoon pure vanilla extract

2 cups sliced strawberries

1 cup raspberries

1 cup blueberries

2 tablespoons sugar

3 tablespoons limoncello liqueur

1 banana, sliced

GARNISH: Fresh mint sprigs

For the lemon yogurt topping, whisk together the yogurt, lemon curd, honey and vanilla; set aside at room temperature.

For the fruit, carefully toss together the strawberries, raspberries, blueberries, sugar and limoncello. Allow them to stand at room temperature for about 5 minutes to let the berries macerate with the sugar and liqueur. Gently fold the banana into the mixture.

Serve bowls of fruit with the lemon yogurt sauce on top. Garnish with a sprig of fresh mint.

lemon ice cream

3 lemons

½ teaspoon lemon extract

2 cups sugar

3 cups milk

1 cup heavy cream

Remove zest from 1 lemon and set the zest aside. Juice the 3 lemons and combine the juice with lemon extract and sugar, mixing until the sugar dissolves. Add milk, heavy cream and grated lemon zest. Pour into an ice cream freezer and freeze according to the manufacturer's directions. Remove from freezer 10 minutes before serving.

CHEF TIP:

SERVE LEMON ICE CREAM WITH A SAUCE OF RASPBERRIES OR STRAWBERRIES. AN ADDED TIP IS TO POUR LIMONCELLO OR GREEN CRÈME DE MENTHE OVER EACH SERVING.

raspberry sauce

1 (10-ounce) package frozen red raspberries, thawed

2 tablespoons red currant jelly

¼ teaspoon fresh lemon juice

3 tablespoons sugar

Dash of kosher salt

1 tablespoon framboise or Kirsch

1 teaspoon cornstarch dissolved in 1 teaspoon water

Heat berries. Add jelly, lemon juice, sugar, salt and liqueur. Bring to a boil; strain, pressing on solids. Return sauce to pan and bring to a simmer. Add cornstarch mixture, a few drops at a time, stirring until desired consistency is reached. Continue simmering for 3 minutes.

strawberry sherbet

6 cups fresh strawberries

2 cups sugar

1½ cups fresh orange juice

½ cup fresh lemon juice

¼ cup orange flavored liqueur

8 fresh strawberries with stems or orange and lemon slices

Wash and hull strawberries. Combine strawberries, sugar, orange juice and lemon juice in a blender, mixer or food processor. Blend well. Add orange liqueur and blend. Freeze mixture. When frozen, remove and beat with an electric mixer. Refreeze until ready to serve. Sherbet mixture can also be frozen in an ice cream freezer, following manufacturer's directions.

To serve, spoon into sherbet dishes and garnish with whole fresh strawberries or orange and lemon slices.

frozen cappuccino demitasse

6 tablespoons instant cappuccino mix, café mocha flavor

6 tablespoons brandy, chilled

1 pint premium coffee or vanilla ice cream, softened

⅓ cup (1 to 1.4-ounce) toffee candy bar, crushed

Whipped cream

GARNISH: 4 cinnamon sticks or cinnamon powder

Combine cappuccino mix and brandy; whisk until mix is dissolved. Fold in ice cream and candy. Spoon mixture into 4 demitasse cups or 4 small ramekin dishes. Freeze at least 1 hour.

Just before serving, top with whipped cream and place a cinnamon stick into each serving or simply sprinkle cinnamon powder over whipped cream.

hot fudge sundaes

Ice Cream and Nuts

Premium ice cream

Chopped nuts (pecans, peanuts, walnuts, almonds)

COMPLIMENTS OF:

CATERER LUCY TOWNSEND

COOPERSTOWN, NEW YORK

Hot Fudge Sauce

¾ cup heavy cream

4 tablespoons butter, melted

Pinch of kosher salt

½ cup sugar

2 tablespoons light corn syrup

2 tablespoons water

9 ounces best quality bittersweet or semisweet chocolate, finely chopped

1 teaspoon pure vanilla extract

With an ice cream scoop, make 4 ice cream balls; roll in chopped nuts to cover. Freeze until ready to serve.

To prepare the fudge sauce, in a measuring cup with a spout, combine the cream, butter and salt. Set aside.

In a medium saucepan, heat the sugar, corn syrup and water, stirring until the sugar is dissolved. Increase heat to high and bring the mixture to a full rolling boil. Cook until a dark amber color, about 1 to 2 minutes, without stirring. Remove the pan from the heat and carefully pour the cream mixture into the sugar mixture. (Take care, since the sugar will bubble up when the cream is added.) Whisk until smooth.

Put the chocolate in a large heatproof bowl. Pour the hot cream and sugar mixture over the chocolate. Add the vanilla and whisk until smooth. Set aside.

To serve, place the ice cream balls in individual dessert dishes and top with warm fudge sauce.

kid-friendly

lemon pecan drops

Cookies

3½ cups all-purpose flour

1 teaspoon baking soda

1 teaspoon kosher salt

1 cup butter, room temperature

1 cup sugar

6 tablespoons fresh lemon juice

3 tablespoons freshly grated lemon zest

2 eggs, room temperature

⅔ cup finely chopped pecans

Glaze

2 cups powdered sugar

3 tablespoons fresh lemon juice

Preheat oven to 350°. To prepare the cookies, line baking sheets with parchment paper or baking mats. Whisk together flour, baking soda and salt; set aside. Beat butter with sugar until light and fluffy. Add lemon juice, lemon zest and eggs; beat well. Add dry ingredients and mix until just blended. Stir in pecans. Drop dough onto pans by heaping teaspoons, placing 2-inches apart. Bake until just set, about 10 minutes. Cool slightly on wire rack.

To make the glaze, whisk powdered sugar and lemon juice. Add additional lemon juice by drops if needed to make glaze run smoothly off the spoon. While cookies are still on the rack, generously spoon glaze onto the top of each cookie.

ginger crinkles

2 cups all-purpose flour

2 teaspoons baking soda

1 teaspoon ground ginger

1 teaspoon ground cloves

1 teaspoon cinnamon

½ teaspoon kosher salt

4 tablespoons butter, room temperature

1 cup sugar

1 egg

¼ cup molasses

Granulated sugar for rolling cookies

Mix together flour, baking soda, ginger, cloves, cinnamon and salt in a large bowl. In another bowl, cream butter and sugar until light and fluffy; beat in egg and molasses. Fold in dry ingredients and chill for 15 minutes.

Preheat oven to 350°. Roll dough into ³/₄-inch balls; roll in granulated sugar. Arrange on nonstick baking sheet. Flatten slightly with the bottom of a small glass. Bake until tops are crinkly, 10 minutes. Cool for 2 minutes on the sheet. Remove to a wire rack to cool completely.

kid-friendly

264 **hearts of palm**

brown sugar shortbread

1 cup butter, room temperature

⅔ cup light brown sugar

2 cups all-purpose flour

Pinch of kosher salt

½ cup unblanched almonds, toasted and coarsely chopped

Cream together butter and sugar until light and fluffy; add flour and salt. Blend by hand until dough comes together and knead the almonds into dough. Gather dough into a ball, wrap in plastic and chill overnight.

Preheat oven to 300°. Divide dough in half. Let sit 10 minutes. On a lightly floured board, roll out dough or press out with heel of your hand into an 8-inch circle about ⅓-inch thick. Place circles on a large buttered baking sheet. Do not have them touching. Score each circle into 8 wedges, prick decoratively with fork. Bake until lightly browned and cooked through, 45 minutes. Let shortbread cool on baking sheet. Cut each circle carefully into 8 wedges.

amaretto butter squares

1 cup butter, room temperature

1 cup sugar

1 egg, separated

1½ tablespoons amaretto or ½ teaspoon almond extract

2 teaspoons grated orange zest

¼ teaspoon kosher salt

2 cups all-purpose flour

¾ cup sliced almonds

Preheat oven to 300°. To prepare the crust, with an electric mixer, beat butter with sugar for 3 minutes until light and creamy. Add egg yolk, amaretto, orange zest and salt. Beat until well blended. Stir in flour and blend again. Pat dough evenly onto a 10 x 15 x 1-inch jelly roll pan. Beat egg white until foamy. Brush evenly over dough and sprinkle with almonds. Bake for 40 to 45 minutes or until light golden. Cool on rack and cut into 2-inch squares.

oatmeal lace cookies

1½ cups butter, room temperature

1 cup brown sugar

1 cup white sugar

2 eggs

½ teaspoon pure vanilla extract

1½ cups all-purpose flour

1 teaspoon kosher salt

1 teaspoon baking soda

3 cups quick-cooking oatmeal

½ cup chopped walnuts

CHEF TIP:

FOR CRISPIEST COOKIES, CUT
BROWN PAPER BAGS AND
SPREAD FLAT ON COUNTER;
PLACE COOKIES ON THE BAGS
TO COOL.

Cream butter and sugars thoroughly. Beat eggs and add with vanilla to mixture. Sift together flour, salt and baking soda. Add to butter mixture and mix well. Add oatmeal and walnuts. Mold mixture into three logs and wrap in plastic. Refrigerate for 24 hours. These will keep in refrigerator for two weeks, or dough can be frozen.

Preheat oven to 375°. Slice logs into thin rounds. Place on oiled baking sheets, at least 2 to 3 inches apart, as they will spread. Bake until brown, checking after 6 minutes. Remove from the sheets immediately, before they start to cool and harden.

coconut-ty brownies

3 ounces best quality unsweetened chocolate

¾ cup butter, room temperature

4 eggs

1 teaspoon pure vanilla extract

2 cups sugar

1 cup all-purpose flour

½ teaspoon kosher salt

½ cup coarsely chopped walnuts or pecans

½ cup shredded coconut

Preheat oven to 325°. Butter and flour a 9 x 13 x 2-inch baking dish; set aside. Chop chocolate into small pieces and put in the top of a double boiler over hot, not boiling, water. Add butter, stirring until melted and smooth. Remove from heat. With an electric mixer, beat eggs for 1 minute. Add melted chocolate mixture, beating constantly; beat in vanilla. Add sugar, flour, salt, nuts and coconut. Beat until combined. Pour into dish and bake 25 to 30 minutes or until a cake tester inserted in brownies is almost clean. Cool on rack and cut into squares.

key lime bars

Crust

5 ounces animal crackers

3 tablespoons brown sugar

Pinch of kosher salt

6 tablespoons butter, melted and slightly cooled

Filling

2 ounces cream cheese, room temperature

1 tablespoon grated lime zest

Pinch of kosher salt

1 (14-ounce) can sweetened condensed milk

1 egg yolk

½ cup fresh lime juice, from 20 Key limes or about 4 Persian limes

GARNISH: ¾ cup sweetened shredded coconut, toasted until golden and crisp

Preheat oven to 325°. Cut an 8-inch wide strip of foil long enough to go down 2 sides and across the bottom of an 8-inch square baking pan, making a sling. Spray with nonstick spray.

To prepare the crust, pulse crackers in the bowl of a food processor to break up large pieces. Then grind until fine. Add brown sugar and salt; pulse to combine. Add butter and pulse until just mixed. Spread mixture evenly across bottom of pan and press firmly. Bake until lightly browned, 18 to 20 minutes.

Work lumps out of cream cheese with a spatula; add zest and salt. Whisk in milk and egg yolk and add lime juice. Pour over baked and slightly cooled crust. Bake 15 minutes and cool for 1 hour.

Run a knife around the edge of the pan. Use the foil sling to transfer cookie to a cutting board. Sprinkle with toasted coconut and cut into 2-inch squares.

cole key nut bars

¾ cup packed dark brown sugar

1½ cups all-purpose flour

½ cup butter, cut into 1-inch pieces

1 (11-ounce) bag butterscotch morsels

¾ cup light corn syrup

4 tablespoons butter

2 (9.5-ounce) cans select nuts (almonds, pecans and cashews)

Preheat oven to 350°. Butter heavily the bottom and sides of a
9 x 13 x 2-inch glass baking dish. Combine sugar and flour in
the bowl of a food processor. Add butter pieces and pulse until
crumbly. Press evenly into prepared dish. Bake 10 minutes and cool
completely.

Melt butterscotch morsels, corn syrup and butter over medium-low
heat, stirring frequently. Remove from heat. Spread nuts evenly over
cooled crust. Pour butterscotch mixture evenly over nuts. Return to
oven for 10 minutes. Cool and refrigerate until set.

To remove from the dish, run a knife around the edge, then place in
a sink with 1 to 2 inches of hot water to soften cookie. Turn dish over
on a breadboard. Cookie should come out in one large piece. Cut
into bars and refrigerate until ready to serve.

walnut squares

Crust

1 cup butter, room temperature

1 cup brown sugar

2 cups all-purpose flour

Filling

4 eggs, beaten

¼ cup all-purpose flour

2 teaspoons baking powder

2 teaspoons pure vanilla extract

2 cups brown sugar

3 cups shredded coconut

2 cups walnuts, chopped finely in processor

¼ teaspoon kosher salt

Preheat oven to 350°. For the crust, combine butter, sugar and flour, using fingers to make a crumbly mixture. Place mixture in two 9 x 9-inch pans or one 10 x 15 x 1-inch jelly roll pan. Pat over bottom of pans. Bake 10 minutes.

To prepare the filling, combine eggs, flour, baking powder, vanilla, sugar, coconut, walnuts and salt. Stir thoroughly. Spread mixture over bottom layer in baking dish. Bake until brown, approximately 20 minutes. Cool. Cut into squares or bars.

Cracker Cottage   Courtney Halpin

The Boca Grande Woman's Club Scholarship Award Recipient

Swamp Cabbage

"A rose by any other name…" might smell as sweet, according to Juliet, but call the delectable hearts of palm by its original Floridian name "Swamp Cabbage" and you are likely to get turned-up noses and no-thank-yous. In reality, according to local history, Shakespeare was right! Picture this: A family campsite in the Everglades in the late 50's, the discovery of a 10 foot Sabal Palm, commonly called Cabbage Palm, the father cutting off the "boots" of the tree, getting down to the core and popping pieces of the tender, white heart into ice-cold water. Everyone, including the kids, would take bites of the raw, delicious vegetable known as "Swamp Cabbage" — a treat as delicate and crunchy and delicious as candy.

Betsy Joiner, a life-long Boca Grande resident, remembers times when the families of local residents and fishing captains would cook the Swamp Cabbage in the kitchen of the "old" Pink Elephant which was owned by her father, Delmar Fugate. The long-lost recipe was called "Martinique Stew" and included kidney beans, chicken, onions and tomatoes. Today we are likely to serve hearts of palm, canned and imported from Mexico or Central America, in an elegant salad. It tastes almost as sweet as Swamp Cabbage.

contributing artists

president's letter

My deepest thanks to the amazing committee which has been immersed in creating this cookbook for many, many months. They have tested and tasted for hours on end. Thanks also to the talented and generous artists of Boca Grande who have donated their works to adorn the pages. Our entire Club hopes that you will enjoy these fabulous recipes.

Leslie Miller

Leslie Miller, President
The Boca Grande Woman's Club

in appreciation

The Cookbook Committee would like to commend and sincerely thank The Boca Grande Woman's Club members, families and friends. Without their commitment to contributing, testing and tasting recipes, **hearts of palm** would not have become a reality.

A special thank you to Alice Gorman, author of the historical vignettes included in **hearts of palm**. These excerpts were drawn from her essay *Boca Grande: Vignettes of History, Myth and Memory*.

The committee also wishes to thank and acknowledge the contributions of these special individuals:

Kim Bax	Tyler Richardson
Tom Bowers	Melinda Rutland
Tanya deBlij	Mary Ann VanLokeren
Bob Green	Toni Vanover
Betsy Joiner	Marjorie Webb
David Pearah	Joe Wier
Julie Richardson Remsen	Vicky Winterer

Our dear husbands: Patrick Carey, John Goetcheus, Ken Richardson

We also apologize to those whose names we may have inadvertently omitted.

testers & contributors

Jennie Albertson

Sharon Allen*

Renae Baker*

Kay Billman*

Doris Bishop

Anne Boomer

Susan Bowers*

Jo Brookhart*

Ginny Bryant*

Pamela Buckles

Cynthia Burcham

Sandy Burroughs

Nella Burton

Jill Butts

Barry Caldwell

Sylvia Campbell*

Jane Caple*

Kay Carey*

Patrick Carey

Jane Carlson

Lois Castrucci

Skipper Christen

Ann Clark*

Mimi Coale*

Jim Cochrun

Leslie Cory*

Bill Craib*

Elizabeth Craib*

Joan Cross

Ellie Cuda

Lois Davis

Bonnie deBlij*

Becky Deupree*

Marsha Dishman

Jan Dunaway

Eleanor Durno

Sue Eddy

Nancy Erb

Danni Ervin*

Florita Field

Beverly Fisher*

Jane Fitzgerald

Jeanne Fleming

Ann Fletcher*

Helen Fraser

Carolyn Frederick

Margo Freeman

Nancy Galliher*

Jane Geniesse

Betty Goddard-Fisher*

Jan Goetcheus*

Connie Gregg

Bunny Hamilton

Corinna Hammond

Cotton Hanley

Donna Harms

Robin Harvey

Lee Havens*

Nancy Hayden

Louise Head

Dodie Headington

Donna Hecker

Gabrielle Heidsieck

Elizabeth Hennenberger

Sally Higgins

Joan Hillenbrand

Dudley Hogue

Anne Honey*

Lynne Hopple

Jean Howard

Maxine Hunter*

Joan Hunziker*

Judy Ikenberry*

Nancy Ireland

Cici Ives

Sandy Jacobs*

Nancy Jaekels

Nancy James*

Susan Jansen*

Thor Johnson

Mary Keevil*

Bebe Kemper

Tooney Kendall

Cassie Kernan

Lona Kissinger

Richard Klepser

Jean Klinges

Audrey Knapp

Alicia Kunisch*

Diane Kunkler*

Ginny Lambrecht

Susan Lambrecht*

Patsy Leggat

Earl Lewis

Elle Lewis*

Donna Lutton

Anne Lyons*

Bette Lyons

Sue Maine

Lindsay Major

Barbara Marmet

Diane Mayer*

Sussie McKean

Nancy Miles

Pam Miles

Leslie Miller

Jane Moore

Marjorie Moore*

Jan Myers*

Al Nethery

Jackie Nicholson

Becky Nidiffer*

Mary O'Bannon

Jane Oliver

Cathy Parkes

Jane Pasman

Sally Pentecost

DeeAnn Phillips*

Je-Je Pierce*

Gail Radey

Patti Rapoport*

Kay Rembold*

Ann Day Reynolds*

Judi Richardson*

Julie Richardson Remsen

Gina Riddiford

Twink Robbins

Linda Roberts

Marcia Rose*

Ruth Ross*

Sue Ryan

Connie Sayer*

Jane Schlegel*

Christian Scott-Hansen*

Louise Scott*

Ann Shaw

Lee Shinners

Nancy Siegel*

Carol Stewart

Margot Stoehr

Dottie Stover

Betty Terrell

Marilyn Thurner*

Carol Tilley*

Boots Tolsdorf*

Ellen Corge Umlauf*

Julie Wahoff

Valerie Walch*

Cappy Warner

Polly Watson

Marjorie Webb*

Jo Ann Welch*

Bebe Wesselmann*

Priscilla Wilcox

Camille Williams*

Loraine Williams

Ann Keefe Wilson*

Mary Jo Wilson*

Bill Winterer

Vicky Winterer*

Toni Wolcott

Jean Wood

*Denotes Testers

notes

index

THE BOCA GRANDE WOMAN'S CLUB
To order copies of **hearts of palm**,
visit our website
www.bocagrandecookbook.com